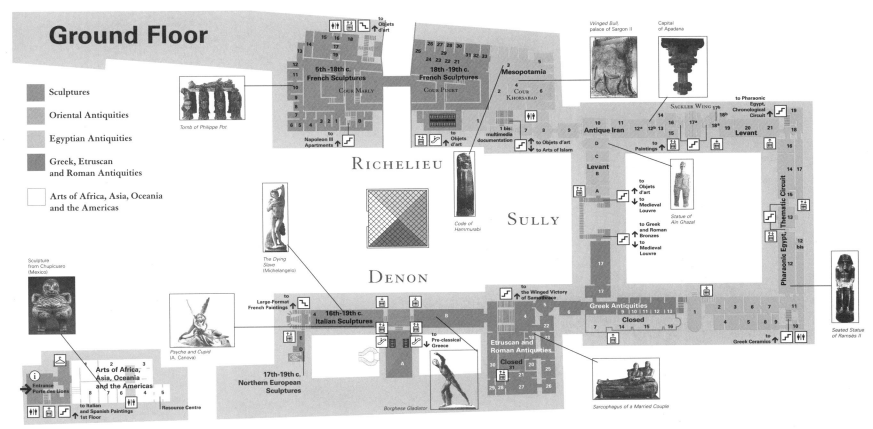

Ground Floor

Sculptures

Oriental Antiquities

Egyptian Antiquities

Greek, Etruscan and Roman Antiquities

Arts of Africa, Asia, Oceania and the Americas

to Objets d'art

15 16 18
14 17
13 19

12
11
5th -18th c.
10 **French Sculptures**
Cour Marly
9
8
7
6 5 4 3 2 1 B

to Napoleon III Apartments

Tomb of Philippe Pot

26 27 28 30
25 31 32 33
24 23 22 21
29
18th -19th c.
French Sculptures
Cour Puget

1 bis: multimedia documentation

to Objets d'art

to Objets d'art
to Arts of Islam

Mesopotamia
3 5
4
2 Cour 6
Khorsabad
1

Winged Bull, palace of Sargon II

Capital of Apadana

Richelieu

Sully

Code of Hammurabi

Sackler Wing 17ᵇ

to Pharaonic Egypt, Chronological Circuit

Antique Iran
10 11 12ᵃ 12ᵇ 13
15

14 16 17ᵃ 18ᵃ 19
18ᵇ
20 **Levant**
21 18
19

16
Levant
B
C
D

to Paintings

to Objets d'art
to Medieval Louvre

Statue of Ain Ghazal

14 17
15
13

12 bis
12

Pharaonic Egypt, Thematic Circuit

to Greek and Roman Bronzes
to Medieval Louvre

17

17

to the Winged Victory of Samothrace

Sculpture from Chupicuaro (Mexico)

The Dying Slave (Michelangelo)

Denon

16th-19th c.
Italian Sculptures

to Large-Format French Paintings

Psyche and Cupid (A. Canova)

E
D
A

to Pre-classical Greece

17th-19th c.
Northern European
Sculptures

Borghese Gladiator

5
4
22
18 23
30 20
Etruscan and
Roman Antiquities
Closed
31
25
29 28 21 27 26

Greek Antiquities
9 10 11 12 13
Closed
14 15 16

1 2 3 4 5 11
6 7 8 9 10

to Greek Ceramics

Seated Statue of Ramsés II

Sarcophagus of a Married Couple

i
Arts of Africa,
Asia, Oceania
and the Americas
1 2 3
4
8 7 6 5

Entrance
Porte des Lions

to Italian and Spanish Paintings 1st Floor

Resource Centre

Louvre
The 300 masterpieces

Louvre
The 300 masterpieces

Text by Frédéric Morvan

HAZAN

MUSÉE DU
LOUVRE
ÉDITIONS

CONTENTS

FOREWORD > 7

A HISTORY OF THE LOUVRE: PALACE AND MUSEUM > 8

NEAR EASTERN ANTIQUITIES > 12
MESOPOTAMIA, IRAN, LEVANT, PRE-ISLAMIC ARABIA

EGYPTIAN ANTIQUITIES > 24

GREEK, ETRUSCAN, AND ROMAN ANTIQUITIES > 40

ISLAMIC ART > 56

DECORATIVE ARTS > 62

SCULPTURES > 76

PAINTINGS > 92

PRINTS AND DRAWINGS > 144

ARTS OF ASIA, AFRICA, OCEANIA, AND THE AMERICAS > 154

PHOTO CREDITS > 158

To provide a compendium of one of the largest and most prestigious museums in the world is an ambitious undertaking. The Louvre, which started life as a fortress in the Middle Ages and became the palace of the kings of France, has for eight centuries provided a sumptuous backdrop for French history. Today, it is a state-of-the-art museum and a thriving cultural center. Its collections, put together since the time of Charles V and above all François I, were opened to the public in an encyclopedic spirit in 1793 and are still evolving. A selection of works from Asia, Africa, Oceania, and the Americas loaned by the Musée du Quai Branly has been on display since 2000, while in 2003 a new Department of Islamic Art was added to the seven existing departments (Near Eastern Antiquities; Egyptian Antiquities; Greek, Etruscan, and Roman Antiquities; Paintings; Sculptures; Decorative Arts; and Prints and Drawings).

These extraordinarily rich holdings, totaling over 300,000 items, include world-famous masterpieces and key works in the history of art and mankind. Our permanent aim is to ensure the conservation of these works and to render them accessible to the public. Visiting a museum should be a pleasure not a duty, because art, ancient or modern, is a vital component of our everyday lives. The challenge for the Louvre is to provide its seven million visitors each year with a faithful account of a story that begins some 10,000 years ago and ends in the mid-nineteenth century. Which works should visitors see? What should they learn? These are questions that this book, thanks to its representative selection from the Louvre's diverse collections, attempts to answer. By placing over three hundred major works in their historical context, it will provide you with a better understanding of the artistic movements out of which they grew. With its aid, you will take away an unforgettable memory of the Louvre's riches with you.

HENRI LOYRETTE
President and Director of the Musée du Louvre

A HISTORY OF THE LOUVRE: PALACE AND MUSEUM

HUBERT ROBERT (1733-1808)
< THE GRANDE GALERIE AT THE LOUVRE IN 1794-96

France, c. 1801-5
Oil on canvas, h. 37 cm, w. 46 cm

Hubert Robert, one of the Louvre's resident artists and Garde des Tableaux du Roi, witnessed the changes made to the Grande Galerie. He painted this true-to-life view and also an imaginary depiction of the gallery in ruins.

ISRAEL SILVESTRE (1621-1691)
∨ CONSTRUCTION OF THE LOUVRE COLONNADE

Engraving

Colbert invited architects to submit plans for the east facade of the Louvre in 1665. The design of Italian Baroque architect Bernini was initially chosen, but in the end the majestic Colonnade housing the royal apartments, which would become a symbol of French Classical architecture, was built by a team of architects including Claude Perrault.

MASTER OF SAINT-GERMAIN-DES-PRÉS
< PIETÀ

France, c. 1500
Oil on wood, h. 97 cm, w. 198 cm

The Saint-Germain-des-Prés Pietà, painted around 1500, is one of the very few surviving depictions of the medieval Louvre. The fortress, which Charles V had transformed into a royal residence in the second half the fourteenth century, is seen here from the left bank of the Seine.

Palace of kings and temple of the arts: this has been the dual vocation of the architectural complex known today as the Louvre, whose history spans over eight centuries. Its origins date back to the late twelfth century, when Philippe Auguste decided to protect his new capital, Paris, by surrounding it with ramparts and building a royal fortress on the right bank of the Seine. This castle's keep became a symbol of monarchic power, but soon lost its strategic vocation as a royal treasure house and prison. The remains of the medieval Louvre are open to the public and accessible directly from the museum's entrance hall beneath the Pyramid, symbol of the modern Louvre.

In the 1360s, King Charles V transformed the Louvre into a royal residence, giving it a decor befitting a king and installing his rich library of manuscripts. But the palace subsequently lost its royal function and it was not until the sixteenth century that another monarch, François I, took up residence in the Louvre. He had the Grosse Tour ("Big Tower") demolished in 1528 and in 1546 entrusted his architect, Pierre Lescot, with the building of a palace in the contemporary Renaissance style. While Henri II pursued this project, his wife, Catherine de Médicis, decided to build a new chateau outside its walls, the Tuileries. In 1566, Charles IX undertook the construction of a long "riverside" gallery linking the two buildings, along

the lines of the *uffizi* of the Palazzo Pitti in Florence. This was the first stage in what would later become the Petite Galerie and Grande Galerie. Henri IV, who would make Paris the political and intellectual center of his kingdom, had plans to considerably enlarge the Louvre, a "grand design" that would only be completed in the seventeenth and eighteenth centuries. Louis XIII entrusted the architect Lemercier with the task of quadrupling the size of the Cour Carrée on the site of the medieval castle and he asked Nicolas Poussin to decorate the Grande Galerie.

Before moving his court to Versailles, Louis XIV instigated a new phase of construction, under the direction of architect Louis Le Vau. A commission of experts, which included Claude Perrault, was chosen for the "Colonnade," the grandiose eastern facade facing the city that is one of the masterpieces of French Classical architecture. Le Nôtre designed the gardens of the Tuileries palace, which housed the royal apartments and a theater, the Salle des Machines. The Galerie d'Apollon, on the first floor of the Petite Galerie, was furnished and decorated by Le Brun. It was restored to its original splendor in 2004.

Artists and craftsmen working for the crown had been living and working in the palace since Henri IV's reign, and Louis XIV had installed the academies of painting, sculpture, and architecture there. But it was Louis XVI who finally agreed to open the royal collections to the public. Inaugurated on August 10, 1793, at the height of the Revolution, the Muséum Central des Arts became a showcase for the former treasures of the crown and works of art seized from the aristocracy and the Church. Artistic booty seized during Napoleon Bonaparte's campaigns in Germany, Belgium, and Italy, complemented during the Restoration by acquisitions and the fruits of archaeological excavations, considerably enriched a collection whose encyclopedic ambition encompassed the "distant worlds" then being discovered.

Henri IV's "grand design" was finally completed by Napoleon III in the second half of the nineteenth century. The Louvre was now shared by the museum and government ministries—the Tuileries palace had been the true seat of power since 1789, which is why it was burned down during the Paris Commune in 1871 and demolished in 1882 by a republican government keen to do away with all symbols of monarchy. All that remains of the Tuileries palace today are the two pavilions at its western corners and the Tuileries gardens, whose central avenue is continued by the Champs-Elysées. The gardens have been restored and are today the home of a major open-air sculpture collection.

The ambitious "Grand Louvre" project launched by President François Mitterand in 1981 is confirmation of the preeminent role of the museum in public life. The reorganization of the palace's interior—the former royal apartments, old museum galleries, and former offices of the Finance Ministry—was undertaken by a team of architects led by the Chinese-born American architect I. M. Pei. His Pyramid above the monumental entrance hall has

become the symbol of one of the greatest museums in the world.

The museum's collections and various amenities now take up most of the palace. The collections of Near Eastern, Egyptian, Greek, and Roman antiquities are largely housed on the lower ground floors and ground floors of the museum's three wings—Richelieu to the north, Sully to the east, and Denon to the south. The sculpture collections are divided between the courts of the Richelieu wing (French) and the Denon wing (foreign). The Department of Decorative Arts occupies much of the first floor of the Richelieu wing and the Galerie d'Apollon. The Department of Paintings is spread over the Grande Galerie, the large red rooms on the first floor of the Denon wing, and the second floor of the Sully wing around the Cour Carrée.

The decoration of many rooms evokes the Louvre's own history: the remains of the medieval Louvre beneath the Cour Carrée; the Salle des Caryatides, a grand reception room during the Renaissance that is now home to Hellenistic sculpture; the apartments in the Pavillon du Roi, where the ceiling of Henri II's antechamber was decorated by Georges Braque; Anne of Austria's summer apartments on the ground floor of the Petite Galerie, given over to Roman sculpture; the paneled rooms in the Colonnade wing devoted to masterpieces of Egyptian art, and the Napoleon III apartments in the Richelieu wing. Other parts were designed as exhibition spaces from the outset, such as the rooms of the Musée Charles-X, whose painted decoration evokes the history and rediscovery of the civilizations of antiquity, and the covered courts housing vestiges of ancient Khorsabad and outdoor sculpture from the seventeenth to the nineteenth century. The Louvre is today a huge museum complex housing historic

collections, as well as spaces dedicated to contemporary artistic expression. It is no longer limited to the gigantic buildings running along the Seine: the works in the Tuileries gardens perfectly complement the sculpture collections, just as the Musée Eugène Delacroix, in the nearby Saint-Germain-des-Prés quarter, complements the paintings collection. Built in 1857 to the artist's specifications, this remarkably well-preserved studio was turned into a national museum in 1971 and became part of the Louvre in 2004.

VICTOR JOSEPH CHAVET (1822-1906)
∧ **NAPOLEON III'S LOUVRE**

France, 1857
Oil on canvas, h. 2.12 m, w. 2.22 m

Henri IV's vision of a series of wings and courtyards linking the Louvre and the Tuileries palace became a reality during Napoleon III's reign. But his dream was to be short-lived: the Tuileries was burned down during the Paris Commune, in May 1871.

> **I. M. PEI'S PYRAMID AND THE COUR NAPOLÉON**

The Grand Louvre project, begun in 1981, involved reorganizing the entire museum around a central entrance hall beneath a glass pyramid in the Cour Napoléon. This final metamorphosis and the museum's new symbol were designed by the American architect I. M. Pei.

VIEW OF THE TUILERIES GARDENS

The 28-hectare Tuileries gardens provide one of the most beautiful walks in Paris. Designed by André Le Nôtre for Louis XIV in 1664 around a long central avenue leading to the Place de la Concorde and continued by the Champs-Élysées, it is now the outdoor home of part of the Louvre's sculpture collection.

MUSÉE EUGÈNE DELACROIX
DELACROIX'S STUDIO

Delacroix's studio, designed by the painter himself in 1857, has a large window overlooking a garden. He lived there until he died in 1863, and it was thanks to his pupils Maurice Denis and Paul Signac, among others, that it was preserved and finally turned into a museum.

CODE OF HAMMURABI

First Babylonian dynasty, reign of
Hammurabi (1792-1750 B.C.)
Found at Susa, Iran;
origin: Mesopotamia, Iraq
Basalt, h. 2.25 m

This tall stele was discovered with other
Mesopotamian war booty at Susa. The king
of Babylon is portrayed at the top
listening to the god Shamash, who is sitting
on a throne in the form of a temple.
The text, written in cuneiform script, is a
code of laws regulating every aspect of
daily life from agriculture, medicine,
and family affairs to theft, false evidence,
and assault and battery, the punishments
for which vary according to the social status
of the guilty party. The principle of "an eye
for an eye, a tooth for a tooth" was adopted
by the Jews exiled in Babylon.

NEAR EASTERN ANTIQUITIES

MESOPOTAMIA, IRAN, LEVANT, PRE-ISLAMIC ARABIA

TABLET WITH PICTOGRAPHIC WRITING

Late 4th millennium B.C.
Lower Mesopotamia
Limestone, h. 5 cm, w. 4.2 cm

The invention of writing in around 3200 B.C., encouraged by trade links and the establishment of administrations in the city-states, was one of the major advances of Mesopotamian civilization. This tablet displays identifiable graphic symbols (for example, the hand) and more schematic marks (the sign for "large," bottom right). They form a coherent text that can be read from beginning to end. These early pictograms would evolve into the complex Sumerian cuneiform script.

The term Near Eastern antiquities encompasses works from the present-day Middle East, the vast territory that was unified under the powerful Persian empire of Darius and finally conquered by Alexander the Great. Stretching from the Mediterranean to the Indus, it was the crucible of the first village settlements, the invention of ceramics in the seventh millennium B.C., and the first city-states in the fourth millennium B.C. It was also the cradle both for the invention of writing and the birth of the first Western religions. The collections of the Department of Near Eastern Antiquities perfectly illustrate the quality of the arts and techniques that contributed to the development of a universal formal vocabulary, which the Greco-Roman world inherited.

From the Neolithic period, the great geographic, ethnic, and linguistic diversity of the cultures of the ancient Orient was marked by the development of commercial, intellectual, and religious exchanges that contributed to the development of a complex civilization. The royal and religious art of these refined cultures is characterized by its anthropomorphism and close link with the forces of nature, which gave rise to a rich pantheon of gods. Throughout the ancient Orient one finds in-the-round and bas-relief depictions of praying figures, deities identifiable by their symbols—the sun, moon, fantastic monsters, genies, and demons—and also representations of ritual libations, offerings, and sacrifices. Sovereigns also had immortalized in stone their war exploits, activities as legislators and administrators, and role as intermediary between the world of the gods and that of man. The ceramics preserved in tombs reveal facets of daily life, while precious metalwork, ivories, and earthenware provide a glimpse of the splendor of court life. Architecture has also survived in the spectacular remains of temples and palaces, ranging from their foundation stones to the great capitals and friezes of the palace of Darius at Susa, the winged, human-headed bulls guarding the palace at Khorsabad, and the mural paintings at Mari and Tel Barsip.

Remains of the cradle of Mesopotamian civilization were not discovered until the nineteenth century, in Iraq, on the broad, fertile plain irrigated by the Tigris and Euphrates rivers. The cities of Khorsabad and Telloh (ancient Girsu) were the first to yield treasures from the civilizations of Assyria and Sumer. They were followed by discoveries in Syria and Lebanon, cradle of Phoenician culture, and in Iran, in the city of Susa, successively capital of the Elamite and Persian empires. Also unearthed at Susa was the "Mesopotamian booty," historic monuments looted by an Elamite conqueror in the twelfth century B.C., including the Code of Hammurabi, king of Babylon (eighteenth century B.C.). These enabled the piecing together of the history of the great empires of Akkad, which included the lands of Sumer, Akkad, and northern Mesopotamia in the third millennium B.C., of Babylon, of Assyria, which reached its height under Sargon and Ashurbanipal, and of the Persians, which Cyrus II the Great and Darius extended into Egypt and to the borders of Greece and India.

The first discoveries sent back to France culminated in the creation of the "Musée Assyrien" in 1847, which in 1881 became the Département des Antiquités Orientales of the Musée du Louvre. The department later grew into a first-rate collection thanks to agreements with several Near Eastern countries and regular private donations. Rich in masterpieces and comprehensive enough to provide a continuous overview spanning several millennia up until the Islamic conquest, it is presented in the museum's Richelieu and Sully wings, organized by geographical area: Mesopotamia, Iran, Anatolia, the Levant, and pre-Islamic Arabia.

AKKAD DYNASTY, REIGN OF NARAM-SIN (2254-2218 B.C.)
FOUND AT SUSA, IRAN; ORIGIN: MESOPOTAMIA, IRAQ
LIMESTONE, H. 2 M, W. 1.05 M

In the middle of this victory stele, one of the most important of the Mesopotamian monuments taken to Susa in the twelfth century B.C., the king of Akkad is shown leading an attack on the Lullubi, a mountain people. As was the convention, he is portrayed larger than his troops and wearing a horned tiara, headdress of the Mesopotamian gods. The stars above the scene, emblems of the great divinities, the sun, moon, and planet Venus, are protecting the royal victory.

^ "STELE OF THE VULTURES"

EARLY DYNASTIC III (2600-2330 B.C.)
TELLOH (ANCIENT GIRSU), SUMER (MESOPOTAMIA, IRAQ)
LIMESTONE, H. 1.8 M, W. 1.3 M

This stele is a work of exceptional historical importance, both on account of the quality of its reliefs and the Sumerian text accompanying them. The oldest known victory monument, it commemorates the triumph of Eannatum, king of Lagash and grandson of Ur-Nanshe, over the neighboring city of Umma around 2450 B.C., after a conflict lasting several generations. On one side, the god Ningirsu is shown seizing enemies in a net. On the historic side, the corpses of slain enemies are being devoured by vultures.

⌄ PERFORATED RELIEF OF UR–NANSHE, KING OF LAGASH

EARLY SUMERIAN PERIOD (2600-2330 B.C.)
TELLOH (ANCIENT GIRSU), SUMER (MESOPOTAMIA, IRAQ)
LIMESTONE, H. 39 CM, W. 46.5 CM

This commemoration plaque depicts the king of Lagash ceremonially laying the foundations of a temple to the great god Ningirsu. The arrangement of the scenes in registers is characteristic of the art of the first Sumerian dynasties. At the top, the king, wearing a *kaunakes*, a skirt with overlapping tufts of wool, is carrying a basket of bricks on his head. At the bottom we see him presiding over a ritual banquet, goblet in hand. This type of perforated relief was probably pegged to the wall.

> ## STATUE OF A STANDING FIGURE

7TH MILLENNIUM B.C.
AIN GHAZAL (JORDAN)
CALCINATE GYPSUM, H. 1.05 M
ON LOAN FROM THE JORDANIAN DEPARTMENT OF ANTIQUITIES

The statue, the oldest in the Louvre, was modeled in plaster
obtained by heating gypsum. It comes from the Ain Ghazal
("Spring of the Gazelles") site near Amman, where it had
been buried with other similar effigies. These standing
figures, dressed and wearing wigs, probably represented
clan chiefs honored during a ceremony. This one has kept
its very expressive eyes, outlined by black bitumen
in a triangular face contrasting with the simplicity
of the massive body.

> ## EBIH-IL, SUPERINTENDENT OF MARI

C. 2400 B.C.
MARI, MIDDLE EUPHRATES (MESOPOTAMIA, SYRIA)
ALABASTER, EYES INSET WITH SHELL, LAPIS LAZULI,
AND BITUMEN, H. 52.5 CM, W. 20.6 CM

Superintendent Ebih-il, an important dignitary
in the kingdom of Mari, is portrayed in the Sumerian
manner then customary in Syria. He is sitting on a
wickerwork chest, a sign of his office, and wearing
the *kaunakes*, the traditional woolen skirt. The statue
is dedicated to Ishtar, goddess of love and war.

< ## STATUETTE OF HAMMURABI
KNEELING IN PRAYER

1ST BABYLONIAN DYNASTY,
REIGN OF HAMMURABI (1792-1750 B.C.)
LARSA, MESOPOTAMIA (IRAQ)
BRONZE, SILVER, GOLD, H. 19.5 CM

This statuette of a man kneeling in
adoration was dedicated to the god
Amurru "for the life of Hammurabi"
by Awil-Nannar, a dignitary of the town
of Larsa, which had just been conquered
by the Babylonians. It portrays the king
himself, wearing the royal hat. He is also
shown on the base, praying before a
god seated on a throne.

> ## GUDEA WITH A FLOWING VASE

2ND DYNASTY OF LAGASH,
REIGN OF GUDEA (2125-2110 B.C.)
TELLOH (ANCIENT GIRSU), SUMER (MESOPOTAMIA, IRAQ)
CALCITE, H. 62 CM, W. 25.6 CM

Many effigies of this prince of Lagash
have been found. He initiated the Sumerian
revival after the fall of the Akkadian
empire and founded numerous temples
in which votive statuettes like this one
were placed. Found in the temple of the
goddess Geshtinanna, it is dedicated to
Enki, god of fertilizing underground waters.

^ **ASHURBANIPAL IN A CHARIOT**

ASSYRIAN EMPIRE, REIGN OF ASHURBANIPAL (668-629 B.C.)
PALACE OF ASHURBANIPAL, NINEVEH, ASSYRIA (MESOPOTAMIA, IRAQ)
GYPSUM, H. 1.62 M, W. 0.77 M

This relief depicts the Assyrian campaign in Elam that
culminated in the fall and pillage of Susa in 646 B.C. It
was part of the mural decoration of a room in the palace
that the king built in his capital, Nineveh. The tall figure of
Ashurbanipal in his chariot and his escort are overseeing
the deportation of defeated Elamites.

< **FRIEZE OF ARCHERS**

ACHAEMENID DYNASTY, 522-486 B.C.
SUSA (IRAN)
GLAZED TERRACOTTA BRICK, H. 4.75 M, W. 3.75 M

The walls of the palace of Darius I at Susa were covered with
glazed terracotta brick reliefs whose purpose was to show
the power and grandeur of the Persian Empire in keeping with
an ancient Babylonian tradition. The marching archers wearing
ceremonial costume in this fragment could be the "Immortals,"
the personal guard of the Great King described by Herodotus.

v **WINGED BULL WITH HUMAN HEAD**

ASSYRIAN EMPIRE, REIGN OF SARGON II (721-705 B.C.)
KHORSABAD (DUR-SHARRUKIN), ASSYRIA (MESOPOTAMIA, IRAQ)
GYPSUM, H. 4.20 M, W. 4.36 M

These huge winged bulls with human heads kept
guard in pairs at the gates of the city and palace
of the Assyrian king Sargon II. They give an idea
of the monumentality of Assyrian architecture.
Like the bas-relief panels and orthostats
that lined the palace's rooms, they testify to
the extraordinary quality of Assyrian sulpture,
which was both realistic yet stylized.

MODEL OF A TEMPLE, KNOWN AS "SIT SHAMSHI"
SHUTRUKID DYNASTY (12TH CENTURY B.C.)
SUSA (IRAN)
BRONZE, W. 60 CM, L. 40 CM

In the middle of this model of an open-air place of worship, two naked men are ritually washing themselves. They are surrounded by a basin for sacred water, bushes symbolizing the sacred tree, and ziggurats (stepped temple mounds or towers). The inscription tells us that this is a "sunrise" ceremony dedicated to the god Inshushinak by the great Elamite king Shilhak-Inshushinak.

^ VASE HANDLE IN THE FORM OF A WINGED IBEX
ACHAEMENID DYNASTY, 539-333 B.C.
IRAN
SILVER, GOLD, H. 26.5 CM

Fine vessels were greatly appreciated at the official court banquets of the Achaemenid Persians. This is one of two handles from a large amphora. The mask of Silenus, borrowed from the Greeks of Asia Minor, and the typically Iranian winged ibex are characteristic of the international style that developed in the Persian Empire.

> BEAKER DECORATED WITH WADING BIRDS, DOGS, AND IBEXES
SUSA I, C. 4200-3500 B.C.
SUSA (IRAN)
PAINTED TERRACOTTA, H. 28.9 CM, DIAM. 16.4 CM

As soon as Susa became capital of the Elamite Empire, a necropolis was established on a terrace above the city. In its tombs, bones were placed in terracotta vases, skulls in dishes, and long bones in beakers. The stylized naturalistic decoration is characteristic of Susan art. The decoration features Iranian mountain ibexes and also sloughi desert dogs, with wading birds evoking the marshes.

∧ STATUETTE KNOWN AS "THE PRINCESS OF BACTRIA"

EARLY 2ND MILLENNIUM B.C.
BACTRIA (IRAN)
CHLORITE, LIMESTONE, H. 18.3 CM, W. 16 CM

This Bactrian princess is wearing a
Mesopotamian-style *kaunakes*, or woolen
braid dress. The use of different materials
enhances the contrast between the light face
and dark green dress and headdress. These
statuettes were placed in temples or tombs
as tokens of devotion.

∨ ELAMITE GOD

SUKKALMAH DYNASTY, EARLY 2ND MILLENNIUM B.C.
SUSA (IRAN)
BRONZE, GOLD, H. 17.5 CM

The horned tiara and long Mesopotamian-
style *kaunakes* indicate the divine status
of this smiling figure. This sumptuous
votive statuette, originally entirely
covered with gold, is perhaps a portrayal
of Inshushinak, "lord of Susa," whose
temple was on the acropolis.

15TH-13TH CENTURY B.C.
RAS SHAMRA (ANCIENT PORT OF UGARIT), SYRIA
LIMESTONE, H. 1.42 M

The storm god, called Baal ("Lord") at Ugarit, guaranteed plant growth and soil fertility. He is brandishing the club from which lightning springs forth to bring rain. The stele illustrates the international nature of the civilization of the Levant, since it owes as much to Egyptian art as it does to that of Anatolia, and anticipates the figures of Zeus and Jupiter in Greco-Roman mythology.

^ MONUMENTAL VASE

7TH CENTURY B.C.
TEMPLE OF APHRODITE, AMATHUS, CYPRUS
LIMESTONE, H. 1.90 M

This enormous three-ton vase is one of a pair made for a temple of Aphrodite at Amathus, near Limassol in Cyprus. The bulls and flowerets on the handles are symbols of the great goddess of Cyprus.

> TRIAD OF PALMYRIAN GODS

FIRST HALF OF THE 1ST CENTURY A.D.
PALMYRA REGION (SYRIA)
LIMESTONE, H. 69 CM, W. 56 CM

The supreme god Ba'alshamin, lord of the heavens, is flanked by the moon god Aglibol and the sun god Malakbel. All three are wearing Roman cuirasses. The trousers and hairstyle of the bearded lord of the gods are both Iranian-influenced and illustrate the cosmopolitan culture of the trading town of Palmyra, located at the crossroads of caravan routes.

< DISH WITH HUNTING SCENE

14TH-13TH CENTURY B.C.
RAS SHAMRA (ANCIENT PORT OF UGARIT), SYRIA
GOLD, DIAM. 18.8 CM

This masterpiece of Levantine precious metalwork
was offered to the temple of Baal at Ugarit. Baal was
the protector god of the city and the reigning dynasty.
The dish is decorated with a hunting scene showing
the king riding on a chariot, followed by his dog.
The game includes wild goats and bovids.

THE GODDESS HATHOR WELCOMING SETI I

**Reign of Seti I (1294-1279 B.C.),
19th Dynasty
Painted limestone
h. 2.26 m, w. 1.05 m**

This large bas-relief from a doorway
in Seti I's tomb in the Valley of the Kings
near Thebes depicts the pharaoh being
welcomed into the world of the dead
by the daughter of Ra. She is wearing
the solar disc within cow's horns on
her head and she is making him touch
her necklace as a sign of protection.
The sumptuous clothes, hairstyles, and
jewelry are all hallmarks of a refined
civilization.

EGYPTIAN ANTIQUITIES

BOOK OF THE DEAD OF NEBQED

18th Dynasty, c. 1550-1295
Painted papyrus, h. 0.30 m, w. 6.30 m

Papyrus scrolls covered with ritual texts and formulae were placed in tombs
to enable the deceased to obtain what they needed during their long journey
through eternity. They were illustrated with vignettes depicting the various stages of
the funeral, mummification, and arrival in the world of the dead, where the soul
was weighed before the god Osiris.

Unlike the mosaic of cultures that characterized the Orient, ancient Egypt retained complete geographic unity and remarkable cultural and political continuity for over 4,500 years. The history of this civilization, indissociable from the Nile and for a long time little known apart from the great pyramids, began to be reconstructed after Bonaparte's Egyptian campaign in 1798 and above all in 1826, when Champollion succeeded in deciphering hieroglyphic writing. The Egyptian department of the Louvre was created that same year, making the museum the first in the world to have a collection of Egyptian antiquities. Thanks to excavations carried out in the nineteenth century by the Institut Français d'Archéologie Orientale in Cairo and by the Louvre, the collection has major pieces dating from the first prehistoric civilizations to the Christian era, and provides a comprehensive panorama of pharaonic Egypt.

Egyptian funerary religion, with its extraordinarily rich polymorphic pantheon, was based on the continuation of life in the afterlife. One of the prerequisite conditions of this immortality was the preservation of the image of the deceased. It was for this reason that tombs have provided a vivid picture of this culture in sacred works and depictions of every aspect of daily life, and in the many texts inscribed in stone and written on papyri or on the deceased's mummified body itself. The world of the dead, on the west bank of the Nile, the side where the sun sets, mirrored the world of the living on the east bank. The Egyptians made use of every material they had at their disposal (stone, clay, bronze) and imported those they lacked: gold from Africa, wood from Lebanon, and also precious stones such as lapis lazuli. In giant granite sphinxes, precious jewelry, and depictions of the pharaohs, their families, and dignitaries, one can follow the progressive elaboration and refinement

of aesthetic canons in the service of the glorification of a people that achieved its goal of living for eternity.

The presentation of the Egyptian collections reflects the universal nature of the works and is divided between two installations in the museum's Sully wing. The first, thematic display covers every aspect of life in the Nile Valley: hunting, fishing, agriculture, and commerce, the arts and crafts, domestic life, writing, temple architecture and decoration, religion and funerary rites. The second, chronological display, from late prehistoric times until the successors of Alexander the Great, contains the Louvre's masterpieces of Egyptian art.

The first dynasties were marked by the establishment of royalty, whose sovereign had a divine dimension. The Old Kingdom (c. 2700–2200 B.C.), which saw the construction of the pyramids at Saqqara and Giza, yielded exceptional works such as the "Seated Scribe." The Middle Kingdom (2033–1710 B.C.) was notable for its excellent statuary and its precious metalwork. During the New Kingdom (c. 1550–1069 B.C.), the golden age of pharaonic civilization, Tutmosis, Amenhotep, Seti, and the Ramesses immortalized themselves with their tombs and great architectural works. The first millennium B.C. was marked by incessant struggles with the empires of the Orient and culminated in the Persian conquest. In 332 B.C., Alexander the Great integrated Egypt into his vast empire and gave it Greek pharaohs, the last of whom was the famous Cleopatra, after whose defeat by Octavius in 30 B.C. Egypt became a Roman territory. The works of Roman and Coptic Egypt are presented separately in the Denon wing, along with works from the Roman and Byzantine eastern Mediterranean.

< GEBEL EL-ARAK DAGGER

C. 3300-3200 B.C.
FLINT BLADE, HIPPOPOTAMUS IVORY HANDLE
L. 25.5 CM, L. HANDLE 9.8 CM

This ceremonial dagger was found in a desert valley
between the Nile and the Red Sea near Abydos. It dates from
the Predynastic civilization of Naqada. The decoration on
the handle shows a "king-priest" holding tamed lions,
a motif of Mesopotamian origin, and combats depicted
in registers—the convention that would become the basis
of representation in the art of pharaonic Egypt.

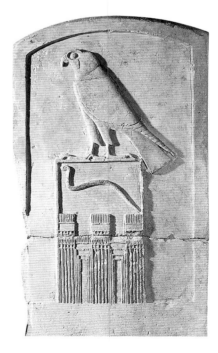

> STELE OF THE SERPENT KING

1ST DYNASTY, C. 3000 B.C.
LIMESTONE FRAGMENT, H. 1.43 M, W. 0.65 M

From the beginnings of Egyptian civilization, the Thinite kings
lavished great care on their tombs. The king, the hieroglyphic
transcription of whose name was a serpent, is protected here
by the falcon god Horus. He was buried at Abydos in a tomb
whose architecture was similar to that represented on this
stele and before which offerings were placed.

> MODEL OF A BOAT

12TH DYNASTY, C. 1963-1786 B.C.
PAINTED WOOD, H. 38.5 CM, W. 81 CM

The tomb of Chancellor Nakhti at Assiut, like all
dignitaries' tombs, yielded much information about
daily life in ancient Egypt, and in particular the important
role of the Nile. In model boats such as this, the deceased
could go on pilgrimages, fish, and even trade and
stock up with food.

< THE GREAT SPHINX

DATE UNKNOWN
PINK GRANITE, H. 1.83 M, L. 4.80 M

This monumental sphinx, guardian of the temple of Amun-Ra
at Tanis in the northwest of the Nile Delta, is one of the
largest now outside Egypt and possibly one of the most ancient.
The sphinx, a lion with a human head, symbolized the majesty
of the pharaoh and was a "living image" of the king, whose
features it was usually given. It also symbolized the sacred
bond with the solar god.

∨ MASTABA OF AKHETHOTEP

5TH DYNASTY, C. 2400 B.C.
BAS-RELIEF, PAINTED LIMESTONE
DETAIL: MUSICIANS

The royal pyramids were surrounded by *mastabas*, tombs
of dignitaries with a crypt containing the sarcophagus. This
one, from Saqqara, is remarkable for the quality and diversity
of the reliefs decorating its walls. They include hunting and
fishing scenes, depictions of work in the fields and livestock
rearing, and also the pleasures of music and dance.

> ### HEAD OF KING DJEDEFRE

4TH DYNASTY, C. 2550 B.C.
QUARTZITE, ORIGINALLY PAINTED, H. 26.5 CM, W. 33.5 CM

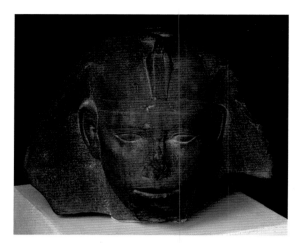

This fragment of a royal sphinx is the portrait of Cheops's son
and successor, and the brother of Khephren. It was found in the
funerary temple next to his pyramid near Giza. The pharaoh's
virile features—high cheekbones and full, sensual mouth—are
sculpted with realism, and he is wearing the royal headdress
in pleated linen, the *nemes*, which is decorated with the *uraeus*,
the archetypal serpent-image of kingship.

^ ### STELE OF NEFERTIABET

4TH DYNASTY, REIGN OF CHEOPS, 2590-2565 B.C.
PAINTED LIMESTONE, H. 37.5 CM, W. 52.5 CM

Princess Nefertiabet, probably the daughter of the pharaoh Sneferu
and sister of Cheops, is conventionally depicted in profile, wearing a
priestess's fur robe, sitting at a table, and surrounded with everything
she might need in her daily life in the afterlife: food, beverages,
makeup, incense, pots, and fabrics. The painted low-relief carving
is extremely delicate.

⌄ SEPA AND NESA

3RD DYNASTY, C. 2700-2620 B.C.
PAINTED LIMESTONE, H. 1.65 M, W. 0.40 M

These life-size statues of a high-ranking couple are among
the oldest to have been found in tombs. They represented
the deceased after their death and thus ensured their life
for eternity. Although their anatomy is still heavy-limbed
and their poses stiff, the gentle modeling of the faces
reveals the hand of a sensitive sculptor.

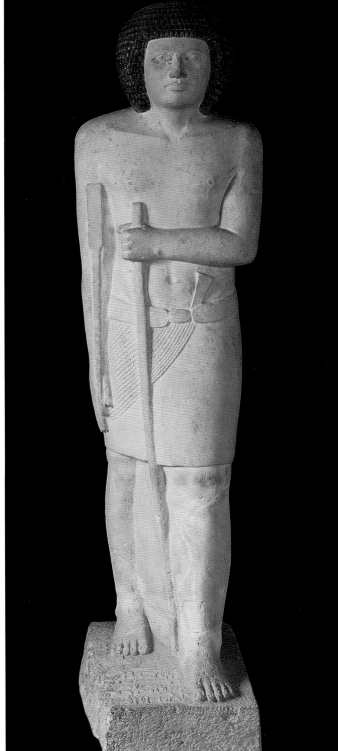

> **"SEATED SCRIBE"**

4TH OR 5TH DYNASTY, 2600-2350 B.C.
PAINTED LIMESTONE, EYES INSET WITH ROCK CRYSTAL IN COPPER
H. 53.7 CM, W. 44 CM

This statue, found in the cemetery at Saqqara, has become
an emblematic work of ancient Egyptian sculpture. Sitting
cross-legged with a papyrus on his knees, this high-ranking
royal dignitary, whose name is unfortunately unknown, is
portrayed with striking realism. The eyes, inset with rock
crystal, and the flesh tones are extraordinarily lifelike.

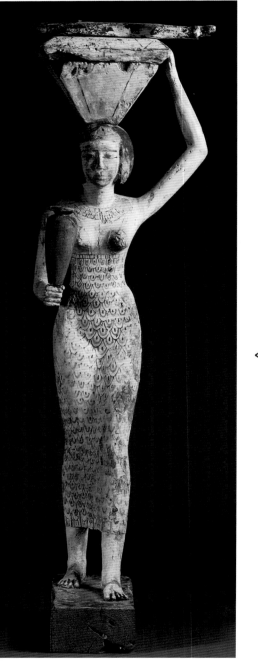

< **OFFERING BEARER**

EARLY 12TH DYNASTY, C. 1950 B.C.
PAINTED FICUS, H. 1.08 M, W. 0.14 M

The tombs of dignitaries were filled with
statuettes of servants accompanying their
deceased master in the afterlife. They provide
a varied picture of daily life. This servant girl,
whose elegant figure is characteristic of the
art of the Middle Kingdom, is carrying a leg
of beef and a water vase.

> **CHANCELLOR NAKHTI**

EARLY 12TH DYNASTY, C. 1900 B.C.
ACACIA, H. 1.78 M, W. 0.49 M

When the tomb of Nakhti was discovered at Assiut, it had
remained untouched for four thousand years after his death
and yielded a remarkable treasure. This statue, surrounded by
numerous servants, was one of the many portrayals of the deceased.
It was sculpted from a single piece of wood and originally
covered with ocher paint. The finesse of the modeling
makes it a masterpiece of Egyptian sculpture.

> ### AMENEMHAT III

12TH DYNASTY, C. 1843-1798 B.C.
GRAYWACKE, H. 21.4 CM

This royal statue conforms to the ideal canon of male beauty in order to express the power of the sovereign, divinity incarnate, but the face of this pharaoh is a portrait of the young Amenemhat III, son of Sesostris III. His features—wide mouth, hooked nose, prominent cheekbones, hollow cheeks, almond eyes—are powerfully and expressively rendered in stone.

^ ### TUYA

18TH DYNASTY, C. 1550-1295
AFRICAN GRENADILLA WOOD
H. 33.4 CM

Tuya, "chief lady of the harem of the god Min," was a high-ranking figure during the reign of Amenophis III. The delicate modeling of the face, the finesse of the details of the wide wig, and elegance of her figure sheathed in a long clinging pleated dress make this funerary statuette one of the most refined pieces produced in the 18th Dynasty.

> ### STATUE OF AMENHOTEP IV

18TH DYNASTY, C. 1350 B.C.
SANDSTONE, ORIGINALLY PAINTED, H. 1.37 M, W. 0.88 M
GIFT OF THE EGYPTIAN GOVERNMENT

Better known as Akhenaton, Amenhotep IV, husband of the beautiful Nefertiti, revolutionized religion and art, and founded a new capital at Amarna. This fragment of a pillar showing the pharaoh holding his royal scepters obeys the new official canon with its androgynous overtones.

∧ RAM-HEADED FALCON

1254 B.C. (YEAR 26 OF RAMESSES II'S REIGN)
GOLD, LAPIS LAZULI, TURQUOISE, CARNELIAN
H. 7.1 CM, WINGSPAN 13.7 CM

This priceless piece of jewelry, found in the tomb of a sacred bull at Memphis, was intended to protect the deceased. Sacred amulets of this type were placed among the bandages during mummification. This one, portraying one of the aspects of the sun god Ra, intercessor between the worlds of the gods and the living, was made using the cloisonné technique with brightly colored stones.

∨ THE GODDESS SEKHMET

18TH DYNASTY, REIGN OF AMENHOTEP III (1391-1353 B.C.)
DIORITE, H. 1.78 M (WITHOUT RESTORED SUN DISC)

This statue, intended for the Theban temple of Amenhotep III and found at Karnak, portrays "she who is powerful," the lion-headed goddess who embodies the destructive forces of the sun god. Responsible for epidemics, drought, and disorder, she was assiduously worshipped to appease her rages and preserve the prosperity of the Nile Valley.

3RD INTERMEDIATE PERIOD (1069-664 B.C.)
BRONZE, H. 95.5 CM

The gods of the Egyptian pantheon could take a number of hybrid forms. Horus is shown here as a falcon-headed man. He would originally have been holding a purifying ewer. The masculine canon of beauty (slender figure, narrow waist, sturdy legs) is masterfully depicted here in bronze. The statue was originally covered with gold decorated with glass paste or colored ceramic.

< THE GOD OSIRIS WITH HIS FAMILY

22ND DYNASTY, C. 874-850 B.C.
GOLD, LAPIS LAZULI, RED GLASS
H. 9 CM, W. 6.6 CM

Monumental despite its small size, this pendant, a masterpiece of precious metalwork, portrays Osiris flanked by his wife Isis and his son, the falcon-headed Horus. The god, a synthesis of Osiris and Ra and guarantor of eternity, is depicted in the position of the solar child being born. He is wearing the *atef* crown and is protected by the woman who brought him back to life to bear him a son.

∧ SEATED CAT

C. 700-600 B.C.
BRONZE, EYES SURROUNDED WITH BLUE GLASS
H. 33 CM, W. 25 CM

The profusion of ex-voto effigies of the goddess Bastet, represented by a cat, attests to her fervent worship, particularly in her town, Bubastis, but also throughout Egypt. A great many carefully mummified cats have also been found. They were sacrificed and then buried in special necropolises.

< KAROMAMA, DIVINE CONSORT OF AMUN

22ND DYNASTY, C. 850 B.C.
BRONZE INLAID WITH GOLD, SILVER, ELECTRUM, H. 52.5 CM

Jean-François Champollion had already been struck by the slender figure and gentle features characteristic of Egyptian art when he acquired this statuette of Amun's wife, "the most beautiful bronze ever discovered in Egypt." The princess, granddaughter of Osorkon I, is shown with the attributes of the pharaoh and would have been holding sistra to awaken the passion of her husband.

> MUMMY

PTOLEMAIC PERIOD, 3RD-2ND CENTURY B.C.
LINEN, PAINTED LINEN, L. 1.67 M

The technique of mummification enabled ancient Egyptians to retain their living form for millennia and was one of the essential components of the cult of life in the afterlife. Evisceration, dehydration, unction, and embalming were the main processes the body underwent before it was wrapped in bandages and protected with amulets.

> SARCOPHAGUS OF TAMUTNEFRET

19TH DYNASTY, 1295-1186 B.C.
STUCCOED, PAINTED, GILT WOOD, H. 1.92 M

In Egyptian religion, the preservation of the
mummy was primordial in ensuring eternal
rest in the "house of eternity." The bodies
of the wealthiest, such as this singer of Amun,
were placed in mummy-shaped coffins fitting
inside one another and painted with symbolic
scenes, texts, and amulets ensuring their
protection and the perpetuation of their name.

< SABINE'S SHAWL

< SABINE'S SHAWL
6TH CENTURY
WOOL TAPESTRY, H. 1.10 M, W. 1.40 M

This canvas shawl decorated with tapestry covered the shoulders of a deceased woman, Sabine, buried at Antioch. The depictions of Daphne and Apollo, Diana the huntress, Bellerophon, and Chimera were inspired by Greco-Roman mythology. They appealed to the tastes of a rich Roman clientele, but the Nilotic decoration of braids is still close to the ancient Egyptian repertoire.

┐ VIRGIN OF THE ANNUNCIATION
LATE 5TH CENTURY
FIG WOOD WITH TRACES OF POLYCHROMY
H. 28.5 CM, W. 14.2 CM

In this group, the Virgin is represented spinning the purple for the veil of the Temple. Of the archangel Gabriel, only one foot has survived. This fragment of a chest or piece of furniture demonstrates the skill of the carvers, despite the rarity of wood in Egypt. Thanks to Egypt's dry climate, the piece has survived in remarkably good condition.

< SOUTH CHURCH, BAWIT MONASTERY, MIDDLE EGYPT
6TH-7TH CENTURY B.C.

Discovered in 1900 by the archaeologist Jean Clédat, the remains of the monastery at Bawit revealed the existence of two churches whose fragments are conserved in the Louvre and the Coptic Museum in Cairo. The Greco-Roman architecture, notable for its remarkable carved decoration, was reinterpreted by local craftsmen and adapted to Christian iconography.

∧ CHRIST AND ABBOT MENA

MONASTERY, BAWIT, 6TH-7TH CENTURY
ENCAUSTIC AND TEMPERA ON FIG WOOD
L. 57 CM, W. 57 CM, TH. 2 CM

A vestige of the Christianization of Egypt, the art of icons differs from the Byzantine influence by their simplicity of composition: Christ places his hand on the shoulder of the father superior of the monastery of Bawit as a sign of protection. The sobriety of the roll that the abbot is holding, possibly the rules of the monastery, contrasts with the richness of the Gospel held by Christ, which is incrusted with pearls and gems.

< EULOGY AMPULLA OF SAINT MENAS

COPTIC PERIOD, 6TH CENTURY
TERRACOTTA, H. 12.4 CM, W. 10.2 CM

From the first centuries A.D., ampullae like this one were sold by the clergy to pilgrims visiting the sanctuary of Saint Menas near Alexandria. They were used to carry water from a miraculous spring, earth from a sanctuary, or oil sanctified by contact with relics. Saint Menas is portrayed between the two camels that returned his body to Egypt for burial.

**APHRODITE OF MELOS,
KNOWN AS THE *VENUS
DE MILO***

c. 100 B.C.
Marble, h. 2.02 m

This statue of Venus, the goddess of love,
was inspired by the figures of Aphrodite
sculpted by Praxiteles in the fourth
century B.C. The spiral posture invites
one to move around her and admire
the full forms of her unveiled anatomy
from all sides. The drapery slipping down
over her hips expresses all the sensuality
of the Hellenistic period.

GREEK, ETRUSCAN, AND ROMAN ANTIQUITIES

The Department of Greek, Etruscan, and Roman Antiquities, along with the Department of Paintings, is one of the oldest in the museum. It covers a long chronological period, from the end of the Neolithic age to the fourth century B.C., an era which saw the break up of the Roman world. It brings together works from all round the Mediterranean that were being collected as early as the Renaissance by humanist princes fascinated by classical culture, such as King François I. His successors enriched the royal antiquities collection, notably through the purchase of the Borghese Collection by Napoleon I in 1807 and the Campana Collection in 1861.

The works in this department, mainly sculpture but also ceramics and bronzework, occupy an important place in the museum. They are displayed in the most prestigious rooms of the former palace of the kings of France: the Salle des Caryatides, the former royal apartments, and the Galerie Charles X and Galerie Campana in the Sully and Denon wings. The heaviest sculptures are on display on the ground floor, while smaller works can be found on the first floor.

The art of the Greeks and Romans has been the model for Western art in modern times, particularly since the Renaissance. That is why we are so familiar with its forms, canons, and mythology, which are all part of our classical culture. The art of these civilizations has survived in a number of materials, including stone, metal, terracotta, ivory, and glass. The evolution of its formal repertoire, based on the quest for an ideal beauty, can be followed in sculpture, architectural decoration, painted ceramics, and precious metalwork. The depiction of the exploits of the gods and heroes of antiquity is the most spectacular testament to a culture less concerned with human resemblance than with the elaboration of sacred canons. Art, used in the service of spirituality, had to illustrate mythology and celebrate the glory of those who distinguished themselves by their virtues. But it also expressed itself in everyday objects, which testify to the refined lifestyle enjoyed by the wealthy inhabitants of Greek and Roman cities.

Initially influenced by Near Eastern forms, Archaic Greek art developed its own original chracteristics and reached maturity in the Classical period. Its zenith was marked in Athens in the fifth and fourth centuries B.C. by the construction of the Parthenon and by the schools of the sculptors Polycletes and Praxiteles. Greek painting, which had almost disappeared, survived in large compositions on ceramics and on steles. The Hellenistic period, which began with the conquests of Alexander the Great in the late fourth century B.C., would infuse severe Classicism with the artistic license of the East to produce a "baroque" style.

In Etruria—present-day Tuscany—a refined civilization blossomed in the eighth century B.C. Etruria's close links with the Greek world brought Rome, which had secured domination of the whole of Italy, into contact with the Hellenistic world. Rome's military conquest of Etruria was accompanied in return by its impregnation by Greek art, which was adapted to the needs of Republican and then Imperial Rome. The Romans also created an official style of portraiture preserving the features of their princes and developed decorative arts such as mural painting, precious metalwork, and funerary sculpture.

< "LADY OF AUXERRE"

C. 630 B.C.
LIMESTONE, H. 75 CM

Is this a goddess, a praying figure, or a servant? The identity
of this statuette from Crete, one of the rare examples of
sculpture in stone from the seventh century B.C., is still a
mystery. The faintly smiling, U-shaped face and stiff, rigorously
frontal pose are typical of the Daedalic style, but the
treatment of volume already foreshadows Archaic statuary.

⌃ WOMEN ON A SWING

CYRENE
HELLENISTIC PERIOD, 323-31 B.C.
LIMESTONE, PAINT, H. 34 CM, W. 28 CM

This metope fragment from the tomb of Altalena is
one of the few examples of painted decoration to have
survived since antiquity. In this charming family scene,
a young woman is gathering her himation before joining
her companion on a swing. Their hairstyles—in a chignon
or short and curled—have red and orange highlights.

> KORE FROM THE CHERAMYES GROUP

C. 570-560 B.C.
MARBLE, H. 1.92 M

This statue from the temple of Hera on the island of Samos,
one of several statues dedicated there by Cheramyes,
is one of the oldest known korai, dating from the Archaic
period. Her body is entirely concealed by a chiton, a heavy
woolen mantle, and an epiblema. The male equivalent,
the kouros, was represented naked.

∧ WARRIOR, KNOWN AS THE "BORGHESE GLADIATOR"

EARLY 1ST CENTURY B.C.
MARBLE, H. 1.57 M

This exceptionally fine statue by Agasias of Ephesus has been famous since its discovery in Italy in the seventeenth century. The expressive figure of this warrior protecting himself from a horseman with his shield is a copy of an original by the great fourth-century sculptor Lysippos, but the mastery of anatomy, volume, and space are Hellenistic.

∨ HERMAPHRODITOS SLEEPING

MARBLE, L. 1.69 M

A Roman copy of an Alexandrian work dating from the second century B.C., this Hellenistic sculpture illustrates the philosophical vision of love proposed by Plato in his *Symposium*. Hermaphroditos, son of Hermes and Aphrodite, joined with the nymph Salmacis to become half male and half female, an ambivalence the sculptor has sensitively conveyed.

∨ HEAD OF A HORSEMAN

C. 550 B.C.
MARBLE, H. (HEAD) 27 CM

Although the torso of this smiling horseman, the original of which is in Athens, retains the conventional frontal position characteristic of Archaic statuary, the sideways movement of the head was a new development. One of the oldest equestrian statues in Western art, it may be a portrayal of the son of the tyrant Pisistrates or one of the Dioscuri, Castor or Pollux.

> TORSO OF MILETUS

C. 480 B.C.
MARBLE, H. 1.32 M

The restrained modeling of this torso is characteristic of the transition between the Archaic and Classical periods in Greek sculpture. Still depicted in a stiff frontal posture, he has his weight resting slightly on one leg. The remarkable treatment of his musculature suggests the movement of the missing arms. Found in a theater, he could have been a depiction of Apollo holding a bow or a dish.

< RED-FIGURE KALYX KRATER BY THE NIOBID PAINTER

C. 450 B.C.
TERRACOTTA, H. 54 CM

With their arrows, Apollo and Artemis are slaughtering the children of Niobe, who had dared to defy their mother Leto. On the other side, Athena and Herakles are shown surrounded by an assembly of warriors. The anonymous painter was named after this major work, which displays great freedom in the arrangement of the figures and their facial expressions.

∨ RED-FIGURE KRATER BY EUPHRONIOS

C. 510 B.C.
TERRACOTTA, H. 45 CM, DIAM. 55 CM

In around 525 B.C., black-figure vase painting was superseded by the red-figure technique in Athenian ceramics, ushering in a golden age during which Euphronios was one of the most prolific painters. The subject here is Herakles' combat with the fearsome giant Antaios. The hero's serene face contrasts with the snarl of the defeated ogre. The scene is framed by two terrified women.

> RED-FIGURE BELL KRATER SIGNED BY THE EUMENIDES PAINTER

C. 380 B.C.
TERRACOTTA, H. 49 CM

In the late fifth century B.C., ceramics workshops in the Greek colonies in South Italy began producing vases of great quality. The theme of this one comes from *The Eumenides* by Aeschylus, in which Orestes goes to Delphi to place himself under the protection of Apollo, who purifies him of the murder of his mother, Clytemnestra, and turns the Erinyes into the Eumenides, or "Goodly Ones."

> ### LARGE KRATER KNOWN AS THE "BORGHESE VASE"

C. 50 B.C.
PENTELIC MARBLE, H. 1.72 M, DIAM. 1.35 M

The Athenian workshops exported huge quantities of these vases decorated with figurative scenes to Italy, where they adorned the gardens of luxurious Roman residences. Their decoration often features Bacchic motifs and is reminiscent of great Hellenistic statuary. In the middle of this composition, Dionysos and Ariadne are surrounded by eight dancing Sileni and Menads.

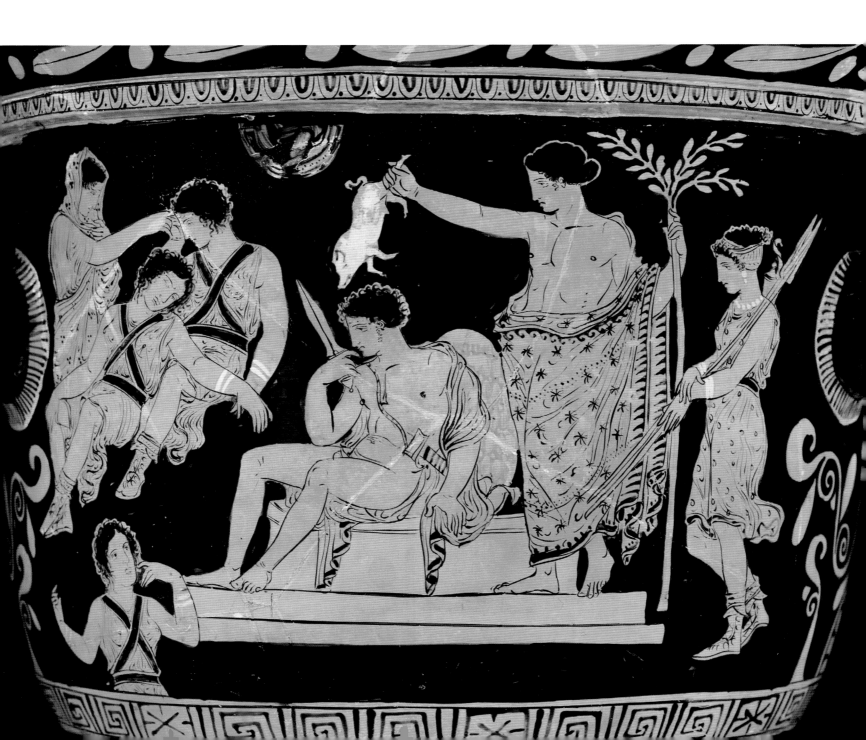

> ## THE WINGED VICTORY OF SAMOTHRACE

C. 190 B.C.
MARBLE (STATUE) AND LIMESTONE (BASE), H. 3.28 M

A monument commemorating a Rhodian naval victory, Victory was originally stood on a base in the shape of a ship's prow in a sanctuary at the top of a cliff. With the billowing wet drapery clinging to her torso and the movement of her outspread wings, this statue, which was influenced by sculptures from Pergamon, is one of the most spectacular works of antiquity.

^ ## "SLAB OF THE ERGASTINES" FROM THE IONIC FRIEZE OF THE PARTHENON

C. 440 B.C.
PENTELIC MARBLE, H. 0.96 M, W. 2.07 M

This fragment is part of the long frieze that ran around all four sides of the Parthenon. The frieze, 160 meters long and containing 360 figures, represents the Panathenaic procession held every fourth year in homage to the goddess Athena. It is one of the major works of Classical sculpture, distinguished by its masterful bas-relief carving and the variety of the poses.

> ## RELIEF FROM A PASSAGEWAY

C. 470 B.C.
THASOS MARBLE, H. 0.92 CM, W. 2.09 M

This relief depicts, on either side of a niche for offerings, three nymphs, still portrayed in the Archaic manner, and Apollo, crowned by another nymph, who is already in the severe Classical style. The figure of the god of the arts displays a concern for movement and suppleness, while the cithara, shown in perspective, suggests spatial depth.

The Etruscans raised terracotta sculpture to
new levels of sophistication. This sarcophagus,
found at Cerveteri (the ancient city of Caere),
is a particularly large example.

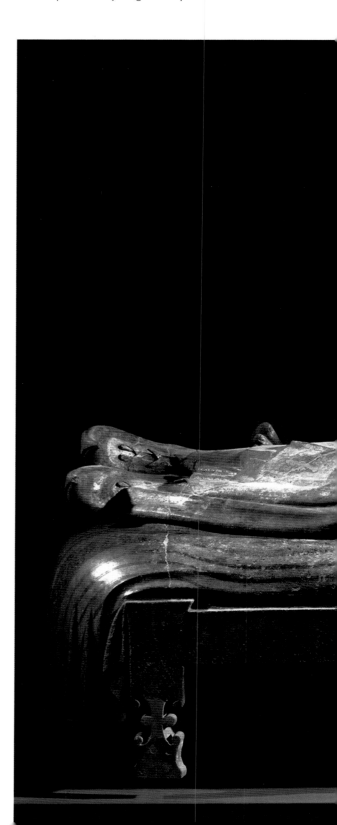

∧ CAMPANA SLAB

C. 530-520 B.C.
TERRACOTTA, H. 1.23 M, W. 0.58 M

"Campana slabs," as they are known, are fragments of wall
paintings from a tomb at Cerveteri (ancient Caere). The face
of the winged being carrying the woman is reminiscent of
motifs from the Greek art being produced in Ionia at the
time, but Etruscan painters succeeded in forging an original
art of their own with a strong sense of movement.

< PENDANT, HEAD OF ACHELOOS
EARLY 5TH CENTURY B.C.
GOLD, H. 4 CM

In Etruscan mythology, Acheloos, the river god of hell, was capable of transforming himself to trick his adversaries. He is depicted on this pendant as a bearded and horned man. This refined piece of jewelry is clearly the product of a prosperous civilization and was made using delicate techniques: repoussé for the face, filigree work for the hair, and granulation for the beard.

^ SARCOPHAGUS OF THE MUSES

C. A.D. 150
MARBLE, H. 0. 61 M, W. 2.05 M

The nine daughters of Zeus and Mnemosyne, together with the philosopher Socrates and the poet Hesiod, are shown here on the front and two ends of this sarcophagus inspired by Greek art. The muses are Clio (history), Thalia (comedy), Erato (love poetry), Euterpe (lyric poetry), Polyhymnia (hymns), Calliope (epic poetry), Terpsichore (dance), Urania (astronomy), and Melpomene (tragedy).

^ FRAGMENT OF THE ARA PACIS (ALTAR OF PEACE) OF AUGUSTUS

C. 9 B.C.
MARBLE, H. 1.20 M, W. 1.47 M

The imperial procession, composed of Augustus and his family, deceased, priests, senators, and magistrates, is modeled on the Ionic frieze of the Parthenon, but features lifelike portraits. It was part of the sculpted decoration for a monument commemorating the emperor's victorious return from Spain, erected on the Campus Martius in Rome, which he had made his capital.

^ MARCELLUS

C. 23 B.C.
MARBLE, H. 1.80 M

Marcellus, nephew of Augustus and destined for the throne, died young. This posthumous portrait by the Athenian sculptor Cleomenes is a combination of Roman realism in the face and an idealized body directly inspired by heroic nudes, in particular the Diadoumenos by the great fifth-century B.C. sculptor Polykleitos. Here, imperial art is referring back to Classical art.

∧ LIVIA
C. 30 B.C.
BASALT, H. 34 CM

This realistic portrait of the wife of the emperor Octavius Augustus aged around thirty and with an early imperial hairstyle is still in the Republican tradition of exalting the virtues of the ruling class. However, its hieratic forms, accentuated by the coldness of the stone, are also reminiscent of the royal art of Greek Egypt, which had recently become a Roman colony.

∧ HADRIAN
C. A.D. 120
MARBLE, H. 48 CM, W. 60 CM

Hadrian, emperor from 117 to 138, reigned over an empire encompassing the entire Mediterranean region and whose diversity was reflected in his villa at Tivoli near Rome. This bust, discovered in Crete, shows his love of Classical Greek and Hellenistic art. He is portrayed bearded, as a philosopher, protected by a breastplate with a Gorgon's mask, but the portrait's realism is distinctively Roman.

^ SILVER DISH FROM THE BOSCOREALE TREASURE
1ST CENTURY A.D.
PARTIALLY GILDED SILVER, DIAM. 22.5 CM

This exceptional silver dish was found near Pompeii, in a villa buried beneath
the ashes after the eruption of Vesuvius in 79 A.D. Its decoration shows a woman,
possibly Cleopatra or the daughter she bore Julius Caesar, but she is also
an allegory for Africa as she is wearing an elephant hide and holding a cobra
and a horn of plenty.

< **"THE JUDGMENT OF PARIS"**

MOSAIC FROM ANTIOCH
C. A.D. 115
MARBLE, LIMESTONE, GLASS PASTE
L. 1.86 M, W. 1.86 M

The murals of Roman villas were complemented by elaborate floor mosaics made in the workshops of the Hellenized East. Inspired by a Greek painter, this centerpiece of the *triclinium* (dining room) of a villa at Antioch, now in Turkey, shows Paris contemplating the three goddesses Athena, Hera, and Aphrodite. The border of leaves and heads is derived from a model from Pergamon.

> **PAINTING FROM POMPEII**

EARLY 1ST CENTURY A.D.
FRESCO, H. 83 CM, W. 1.35 M

The eruption of Vesuvius buried the villas of Pompeii, preserving their wall decorations until they were unearthed in the eighteenth century. The painter of this mysterious fresco, which could be a scene from everyday life or a depiction of a ritual, used his mastery of perspective to create spatial depth.

ISLAMIC ART

^ **PYXIS OF AL-MUGHIRA**

Cordoba, Spain, 968
Ivory, h. 17.6 cm

This casket made from elephant ivory was presented
to a young prince, the son of the Umayyad caliph
of Cordoba in Spain. The refined decoration is
infused with the symbolism of the Umayyads.
Hunting is omnipresent, but there is also a group
of three figures, one playing a lute, another
holding a bottle, and the third a flabellum.

< **THE "MANTES" CARPET**

Northwest Iran, late 16th century
Wool, asymmetric knot, l. 7.83 m, w. 3.79 m

In the sixteenth century, imperial workshops produced
some of the most beautiful "medallion" carpets,
whose composition is organized around a large
star-shaped centerpiece with symmetrical motifs
on either side of a median line. The blue and
red ground accentuates the light hues of scenes
teeming with animals and floral motifs.

The Louvre's collection of Islamic art, one
of the largest in the West, illustrates the
artistic creation of the "classical" Islamic
world, which stretched from Spain to
northern India from the seventh to the
nineteenth century. Although certain
spectacular works such as the "Baptistery
of Saint Louis" were already in the royal
collections, it was not until the late
nineteenth century that an Islamic art
section was created to receive bequests
and donations, together with acquisitions
such as the "Barberini Vase." The opening
of this section was a response to the
new interest in Islamic art and the
contemporary vogue for Orientalism.
The reorganization of the Grand Louvre
enabled the creation of new rooms in
the Richelieu wing to display ceramics,
metalwork, objects in glass, wood,
and ivory, carpets, and manuscripts.
These objects express the refinement
and creativity of Islamic culture, and
reflect the traditions of calligraphy
and geometric patterning. There are
few religious themes in the Islamic arts.

A full-fledged department was
created in 2004, and the collection will
be installed in a larger space in 2008.

Islamic art of the medieval period
is crucial for an understanding of the
heritage of antiquity, and the museum's
collections encompass the Umayyads,
founders of the first Islamic dynasty in
Damascus in the seventh century, the
Abassids of Baghdad, and the Fatimids
and Mamluks in Cairo. In Mongol Iran
and Mughal India, the gates of the
Orient opened onto the Silk Road and
the riches of the great eastern bazaars.
During the Ottoman Empire, which
reached its height under Sulaiman the
Magnificent in the sixteenth century,
elaborate ceramics, carpets, and precious
metalwork developed in parallel with
the decorative arts in Europe.

^ INCENSE BURNER IN THE FORM OF A LION

KHURASAN, 11TH-12TH CENTURY
CAST BRONZE, ENGRAVED OPENWORK DECORATION,
INLAID WITH GLASS PASTE
H. 28.2 CM, W. 32 CM

The antique tradition of metalwork
flourished in Saljuq Iran, particularly
in Khurasan, whose workshops were highly
inventive. Zoomorphic forms such as birds
and wild cats appeared on everyday objects
in ceramic and metal, like this incense
burner with a movable head.

∨ PEACOCK AQUAMANILE

SPAIN, 972
CAST BRONZE
H. 95 CM

This large bronze peacock is an illustration
of the vitality of the Umayyad caliphate
in Spain. The mysterious engraved inscriptions
mention King Solomon (Sulaiman) who,
in Islamic tradition, understood the language
of the birds and had power over storms.

^ BOTTLE BEARING THE ARMS OF TUQUZTIMUR

SYRIA OR EGYPT, MID-14TH CENTURY
BLOWN GLASS, ENAMELED AND GILDED, H. 50.5 CM

Mamluk art—the court art of the sultans and their emirs—
is especially notable for its refined glassware decorated
with cursive calligraphy on a stylized, often floral-inspired
background. This large bottle bears the arms of an emir,
cup-bearer of Sultan Nasir al-Din Muhammad,
future viceroy of Damascus.

Muhammad ibn al-Zayn

∨ **Panel with hunters**

EGYPT, 11TH-12TH CENTURY
IVORY, TRACES OF PAINT
H. 5.6 CM, W. 10.2 CM

This carved and engraved openwork ivory panel features hunting scenes executed in a precise yet dynamic style. Against a background of vine branches, it portrays hunting on foot, in the center, and on horseback, with a falcon and leopard. These Oriental princely pursuits spread to the West after the Islamic conquest of Spain in the eighth century.

∧ **Basin known as the "Baptistery of Saint Louis"**

SYRIA OR EGYPT, LATE 13TH-EARLY 14TH CENTURY
BEATEN BRASS, ENGRAVED DECORATION, INLAID WITH CHASED SILVER, GOLD AND BLACK PASTE, H. 23.2 CM, DIAM. 50.5 CM

This basin, ornately decorated with naturalistic motifs outside and inside was made from a single sheet of brass inlaid with gold and silver. It is thought that Louis brought this masterpiece of Mamluk metalware back from the Crusades. One of the treasures of the French royal collections, it was used for royal baptisms.

MUHAMMAD QASIM-I TABRIZI

< SHAH ABBAS I AND HIS PAGE

IRAN, MARCH 12, 1627
INK, COLOR, GOLD ON PAPER
PAGE: H. 27.5 CM, W. 16.8 CM
MINIATURE: H. 25.5 CM, W. 15 CM

The only known portrait of the fifth
emperor of the Safavid dynasty of
Iran, which made Ispahan its capital,
this miniature shows him in his garden
with a page serving him a cup of wine.
It is accompanied by a short poem:
"May life grant all you desire from
three lips, those of your lover,
the river, and the cup."

^ HORSE-HEAD DAGGER

INDIA, 17TH CENTURY
BLADE: STEEL, DECORATION INLAID WITH GOLD
HANDLE: JADE INLAID WITH PRECIOUS STONES
H. 50.5 CM

The Mughal Empire, founded in 1526,
produced a new and remarkable synthesis
of the Iranian (Timurid and Safavid) and
Indian traditions. Elaborately decorated
daggers such as this one were very popular
with the Mughals.

∧ PLATE WITH FALCONER ON HORSEBACK

KASHAN, IRAN, EARLY 13TH CENTURY
SILICEOUS CERAMIC WITH OVERGLAZE DECORATIONS AND GOLD AND METALLIC LUSTER, DIAM. 22 CM

Overglaze painted ceramics of Saljuq Iran are characterized by their delicate technique, precise designs, and low-fire polychrome decoration with gold luster. They also reflect the influence of the Far East, evident here in this portrayal of a young prince with a falcon on his horse.

> "SHROUD OF SAINT JOSSE"

KHURASAN, IRAN, MID-10TH CENTURY
SAMITE, H. 52 CM, W. 94 CM

This piece of silk, brought back from the first Crusade in 1099, is of considerable historic interest. An inscription in Kufic script invokes glory and prosperity to the Turkish governor of Khurasan. The motifs, inspired by the art of Sassanid Iran, include elephants (a symbol of royalty), Bactrian camels, and dragons.

DECORATIVE ARTS

GRAND SALON OF THE NAPOLEON III APARTMENTS

The Second Empire's Ministry of State reception rooms were decorated from 1856 to 1861 by Hector Lefuel in a sumptuous and eclectic style inspired both by the seventeenth and eighteenth centuries. The decoration of the Grand Salon, which could be transformed into a theater, depicts the history of the construction of the Louvre and Tuileries palaces. The room, occupied until 1989 by the French Finance Ministry, is both a unique testament to imperial pomp and the finest surviving decorative ensemble dating from the Second Empire.

< GALERIE D'APOLLON

Following a fire in 1661, the architect Le Vau rebuilt the upper part of the Petite Galerie and created the Galerie d'Apollon. Its painted and sculpted decoration, on the theme of the sun to glorify Louis XIV, was entrusted to the First Painter to the King, Charles Le Brun. It was restored for the first time in 1849 by Félix Duban, and in 1851 Eugène Delacroix painted *Apollo Overcoming the Serpent Python*. It regained all its original splendor after the restoration completed in 2004 and is now given over to the royal treasures: crowns and diadems, vases, and jewelry, including the famous 140-carat diamond, the "Regent."

The collection of this important department extends from the end of the Roman Empire to the nineteenth century and illustrates the considerable diversity of techniques employed in the production of luxury objects. Formed after the French Revolution, initially with the coronation regalia of the kings of France, the treasure from the royal abbey of Saint-Denis, and the royal collections of bronzes and hard-stone vases, the collection grew considerably in the nineteenth century. Through the acquisition of private collections, it gained magnificent examples of precious metalwork, objects in ivory from the Middle Ages, furniture, tapestries, ceramics, and Renaissance glassware and bronzes. In 1870 and 1901, the Mobilier National enriched the collection with seventeenth- and eighteenth-century furniture, tapestries, and bronze furnishings from former royal and imperial residences. The extension of the collections to nineteenth-century objets d'art and the incorporation of the sumptuous Napoleon III Apartments into the department enable one to follow the evolution from the Renaissance to the eclecticism of the Second Empire.

Now installed in the Richelieu wing, which for many years was occupied by the Finance Ministry, the collection of the Department of Decorative Arts provides a remarkable cross-section of refined taste in Europe, demonstrating the virtuosity of its artists and artisans in the production of both religious objects and luxurious everyday artefacts. Priceless reliquaries and Byzantine, Carolingian, Roman, and Gothic liturgical treasures provide a comprehensive overview of the richness of the Middle Ages. The Italian Renaissance artists' mastery of ceramics and bronze and their humanist culture pervaded all Europe. Tapestry, which spread from Flanders, evokes the decoration of the great houses. The journey into the past continues with seventeenth- and eighteenth-century furniture and prestige objects made by cabinetmakers and metalsmiths, and the products of the royal porcelain and tapestry manufactories. Boulle's masterpieces of marquetry, the furniture of the great cabinetmakers of the century of the Enlightenment, the bedroom and drawing room of Juliette Récamier, and the sumptuous objects that Napoleon I commissioned from Percier, Biennais, and Jacob are high points in the history of French furniture and the decorative arts in general. The Galerie d'Apollon completes the visit.

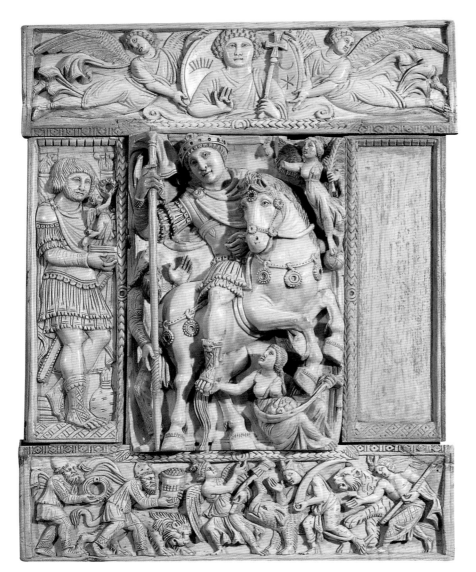

THE EMPEROR TRIUMPHANT, KNOWN AS THE "BARBERINI IVORY"

CONSTANTINOPLE, FIRST HALF OF THE 6TH CENTURY
LEAF OF A DIPTYCH, IVORY, TRACES OF INLAY
H. 34.2 CM, W. 26.8 CM

Consisting of five ivory plaques joined together, this relief is one of the rare vestiges of sixth-century imperial Byzantine art. In the middle, in high relief, is the figure of the victorious emperor, perhaps Justinian (527–65), surmounted by the figure of Christ. The classicism of Greco-Roman sculpture has persisted here in the first Christian art of the East.

SCEPTER OF CHARLES V

PARIS, 1364? AND 1379-80
GOLD (ORIGINALLY ENAMELED), SILVER, PEARLS,
PRECIOUS STONES, GLASS, H. 60 CM, W. 24.2 CM

In anticipation of his son Charles VI's accession to the throne, Charles V had the royal workshops make this scepter as an addition to the royal coronation regalia kept in the abbey of Saint-Denis. The statuette portrays Charles the Great (Charlemagne) to recall the dynasty's Carolingian descent and its legitimacy.

EQUESTRIAN STATUETTE OF CHARLEMAGNE OR CHARLES THE BALD

HORSE: LATE ROMAN EMPIRE OR 9TH CENTURY,
RESTORED 18TH CENTURY
RIDER: 9TH CENTURY
BRONZE, ONCE GILT, H. 25 CM

Although the horse is probably a reused antique bronze, the horseman dates from the ninth century. It is a portrayal either of the Emperor Charlemagne or his grandson Charles the Bald, contemporary descriptions of whom emphasize their resemblance: round face, mustache, bulging eyes. A unique example of Carolingian bronze sculpture, it was formerly in the treasury of Metz Cathedral.

‹ PATEN

STONE: 1ST CENTURY B.C. OR A.D.
MOUNT: SECOND HALF OF THE 9TH CENTURY
SERPENTINE, GOLD, PEARLS, PRECIOUS STONES, COLORED GLASS, DIAM. 17 CM

A priceless vestige of the royal abbey of Saint-Denis, this paten consists of an antique saucer inlaid with gold fish set into a Carolingian mount made of gold decorated with precious stones, pearls, and colored glass. Together with an agate chalice, it formed a set that was presented to the abbey by Charles the Bald.

↵ "SUGER'S EAGLE"

VASE: EGYPT OR IMPERIAL ROME
MOUNT: SAINT-DENIS, BEFORE 1147
RED PORPHYRY VASE, SETTING OF GILDED AND NIELLOED SILVER
H. 43.1 CM, W. 27 CM

It was Abbot Suger of Saint-Denis, regent of the realm during the Second Crusade of Louis VII (1147–49), who enabled Gothic architecture to flourish in the Île-de-France. He considerably enriched the treasury of the royal abbey with exceptional objects, such as this antique vase transformed into a ewer in the form of an eagle.

^ CORONATION SWORD OF THE KINGS OF FRANCE, KNOWN AS THE "SWORD OF CHARLEMAGNE"

SAINT-DENIS, 10TH-12TH CENTURIES
GOTHIC OR MODERN HANDLE;
MODERN BLADE AND POMMEL
GOLD, PRECIOUS STONES, STEEL
H. 1 M, W. 0.22 M

Among the coronation regalia, the sword and spurs were emblems of the king's chivalry. From the eighth century, this sword was thought to be "La Joyeuse," the sword of the Emperor Charlemagne celebrated in *chansons de geste* in the Middle Ages. It was used for the last time at Charles X's coronation in 1824.

VIRGIN AND CHILD OF JEANNE D'EVREUX

PARIS, BETWEEN 1324 AND 1339
SILVER GILT, TRANSLUCENT BASSE-TAILLE ENAMEL, GOLD,
ROCK CRYSTAL, PRECIOUS STONES, PEARLS, H. 69 CM

This reliquary, exceptional in the richness of its metalwork
and enameling, was presented by Charles IV's widow
to the royal abbey of Saint-Denis. The gold and crystal
fleur-de-lis contains the relics of the Virgin Mary. An example
of the Byzantine "Virgin of Tenderness" type, this statuette
has a sinuous pose with the weight slightly on one foot.

∧ VIRGIN AND CHILD FROM THE SAINTE-CHAPELLE

PARIS, THIRD QUARTER OF THE 13TH CENTURY (BEFORE 1279)
IVORY, TRACES OF POLYCHROMY AND GILDING, H. 41 CM

This monumental ivory Virgin and Child is a masterpiece of
Parisian Gothic art, a synthesis of refinement and harmony.
The flowing anatomy, weight slightly on one leg, delicate,
smiling face, and lively drapery are the defining characteristics
of this much admired and imitated model.

> ALPAIS CIBORIUM

LIMOGES, C. 1200
GILDED COPPER, CHAMPLEVÉ ENAMEL
GLASS CABOCHONS
H. 30 CM, DIAM. 16.8 CM

This ciborium, a liturgical vase
designed to hold the eucharistic bread,
is a masterpiece of Limousin champlevé
enamelwork and one of the rare pieces
to have been signed by its maker. The
complex decoration, a combination of
geometrical motifs, figures of angels
and saints, and fantastic animals
on a blue enamel ground, illustrates
the richness of Romanesque art.

> THE TRANSFIGURATION OF CHRIST

CONSTANTINOPLE, C. 1200 OR EARLY 14TH CENTURY
GILT COPPER, MARBLE, LAPIS LAZULI, GLASS, WAX, PUTTY (RESTORATION)
ON A SLATE SUPPORT, COPPER ROD, H. 52 CM, W. 35 CM

This portable icon is characteristic of production in Constantinople
in the twelfth century. Icons, which were intended for personal
worship, illustrated the life of Christ and the saints. This one
depicts the Transfiguration, the occasion when Christ took
three of his disciples—Peter, John, and James—up Mount Tabor,
where Elijah and Moses appeared and Christ was transfigured.

^ THE OFFERING OF THE HEART

PARIS, C. 1400-1410
WOOL AND SILK TAPESTRY, H. 2.47 M, W. 2.09 M

This tapestry was probably made in Arras, a town that produced many such pieces, which were inspired by the courtly, secular literature popular during the Gothic period, particularly *Le Roman de la rose*. The "offering of the heart" was the first step along the amorous path upon which the two lovers embarked. They are depicted here surrounded by domestic animals in a landscape.

LÉONARD LIMOSIN (C. 1505-C. 1575)

^ PORTRAIT OF HIGH CONSTABLE
ANNE DE MONTMORENCY

LIMOGES, 1556
PAINTED ENAMEL ON COPPER, GILT-WOOD MOUNT
H. 72 CM, W. 54 CM

Anne de Montmorency (1493–1567) was the friend and advisor
of Henri II, and one of the great patrons of the French court.
The tempered realism of this portrait and the sobriety of
his dress contrast with the frame, in which all the fantasy
of the Mannerist School of Fontainebleau has been
transposed into Limoges enamel, with a chubby-cheeked
cupid, male and female satyrs, children, and gorgon's head.

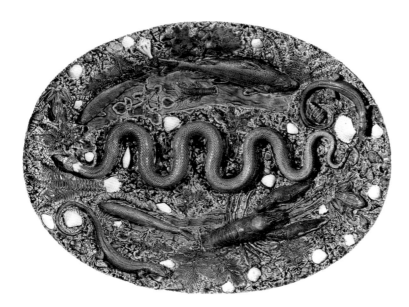

PIERRE REYMOND (C. 1513-AFTER 1584)

^ ROUND DISH WITH BOSS:
MOSES AND JETHRO

LIMOGES, 1569
PAINTED ENAMEL ON COPPER, DIAM. 46.5 CM

Dishes of this kind in grisaille, produced by Limoges
enamelers inspired by Mannerism, were highly sought
after. Their subject matter could be sacred or profane,
such as the months and seasons. The biblical scene
depicted here is Jethro's presentation of his daughter
Sephora to her future husband, Moses.

NICOLA DA URBINO (ACTIVE 1529-1538)

^ PLATE WITH THE COAT OF ARMS OF ISABELLA
D'ESTE-GONZAGA, MARCHIONESS OF MANTUA:
ABIMELECH SPYING ON ISAAC AND REBECCA

URBINO, C. 1525
MAJOLICA, DIAM. 33 CM

Urbino was one of the main production centers for *istoriato* ware,
Italian Renaissance majolica featuring historical, mythical, biblical,
or genre scenes. This plate, made for the Vatican after a drawing
by Raphael (1483–1520), is an example of its quality. It was part
of a service on the theme of Genesis commissioned by the famous
Renaissance patron of the arts, Isabella d'Este, marchioness of Mantua.

BERNARD PALISSY (C. 1510-1590)

< DISH WITH "RUSTIC FIGULINES"

PARIS, C. 1560
GLAZED TERRACOTTA, H. 52.5 CM, W. 40 CM

Architect, writer, chemist, and legendary ceramicist Bernard Palissy
developed a type of pottery called "rustic ware," consisting of
large dishes decorated with reptiles and insects realistically
modeled in high relief. For these "rustic figulines," he made
molds from casts of dead reptiles, using them to make dishes
like this one, as well as grottos such as the one he built in the
garden of Catherine de Médicis in the Tuileries.

ANTONIO PUCCIO, KNOWN AS PISANELLO (C. 1395-1455)

∧ LIONELLO D'ESTE, MARQUIS OF FERRARA

PISA, C. 1450
BRONZE MEDAL, DIAM. 9.8 CM

Best known as a painter, Pisanello was also the inventor of the portrait medal, a commemorative object inspired by an interest in antique coins bearing portraits of emperors. Pisanello made medals for the ruling families of several Italian states, including the Este of Ferrara. Lionello d'Este, marquis of Ferrara from 1441 to 1450, was one of the great patrons of the Italian Renaissance.

BARTHÉLEMY PRIEUR (1536-1611)

∨ HENRI IV AS JUPITER

PARIS, 1600-1610
BRONZE WITH BROWN PATINA, H. 63.5 CM

Despite its small size, this statuette has a monumentality befitting a king. Henri IV is portrayed here as an Olympian Jupiter, and the sculpture's pendant depicts Marie de Médicis as Juno. However, despite the depiction of both sovereigns as mythological nudes, both are faithful portraits.

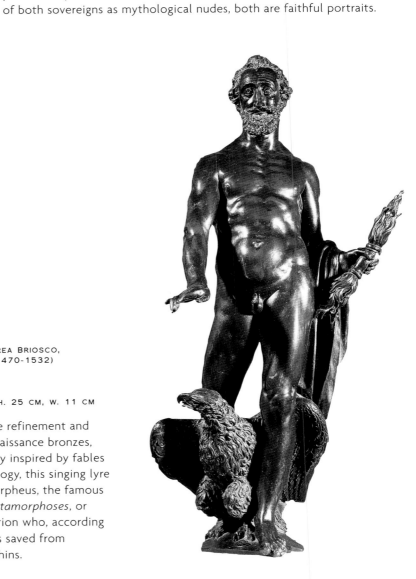

ATTRIBUTED TO ANDREA BRIOSCO, KNOWN AS RICCIO (1470-1532)

< ORPHEUS

PADUA, C. 1510
PATINATED BRONZE, H. 25 CM, W. 11 CM

An example of the refinement and cultivation of Renaissance bronzes, which were usually inspired by fables or ancient mythology, this singing lyre player could be Orpheus, the famous hero of Ovid's *Metamorphoses*, or the Greek poet Arion who, according to Herodotus, was saved from drowning by dolphins.

JEAN BOULOGNE (1529-1608)

> THE ABDUCTION OF DEJANIRA BY THE CENTAUR NESSUS

FLORENCE, C. 1580
PATINATED BRONZE, H. 42.1 CM, W. 30.5 CM

Jean Boulogne, born in Douai, spent his entire career in Florence, where he worked for the Medici family under the name of Giambologna. His bronzes were highly prized. This one, depicting the abduction of Hercules' wife, was offered to Louis XIV by André Le Nôtre in 1693.

< EWER

STONE: 1ST CENTURY B.C.-1ST CENTURY A.D.
SARDONYX, ENAMELED GOLD
MOUNT: PARIS, C. 1630
H. 27 CM, W. 16 CM

This ewer carved in antique stone was one of the jewels of
Louis XIV's hard-stone vase collection. In the seventeenth century
it was given a mount made by Pierre Delabarre, one of the silversmiths
in residence at the Louvre. The handle in the form of a dragon
and the lid with a head of Minerva show the refinement
of the court art of the period.

OTTAVIO MISERONI (D. 1624)

> NEF

PRAGUE, 1608
JASPER, GILDED SILVER, H. 19 CM, W. 58 CM

This exceptionally large centerpiece dish was made in Prague
by a Milanese artist for Emperor Rudolf II (1552–1612) before entering
Louis XIV's collection of vases. It illustrates the Baroque taste
for curios and voluptuous forms, which the engraver enhanced
here with bearded masks.

< NEF

STONE: ITALY, 16TH CENTURY
MOUNT: PARIS, MID-17TH CENTURY
LAPIS LAZULI, GILDED SILVER, ENAMELED GOLD
H. 41.5 CM, W. 33 CM

Every European monarch loved to surround
himself with priceless objects and Louis XIV
was no exception. He amassed a veritable
royal treasure, including this lapis-lazuli nef.
The mount, a tour de force of virtuoso
chasing and enameling, combines floral
motifs and mythological figures: Neptune,
Egyptian sphinxes, a satyr's head, a
shark's head, and grotesques.

FRANÇOIS-DÉSIRÉ FROMENT-MEURICE (1802-1855)

> GRAPE-HARVEST CUP

PARIS, C. 1844
PARTIALLY GILDED AND ENAMELED SILVER, AGATE, PEARLS
H. 35 CM, W. 27 CM

The theme of this extraordinary cup, reminiscent of the Renaissance hard-stone vases collected by the kings of France, is intoxication. The mount is composed of vine leaves and pearl grapes, while the vinestock base is surrounded by figures of Noah, symbolizing the intoxication of wine, Lot, the intoxication of love, and Anacreon, the intoxication of poetry.

ALEXANDRE-GABRIEL LEMONNIER (1808-1884)

^ CROWN OF EMPRESS EUGÉNIE

PARIS, 1855
GOLD, 2,490 DIAMONDS, 56 EMERALDS
H. 13 CM, DIAM. 15 CM

This crown is decorated with eagles and palm leaves (characteristic imperial motifs) and surmounted by an orb and a cross in diamonds and emeralds. Made by Napoleon III's personal jeweler, it escaped the sale of the crown jewels by the Third Republic in 1887.

AUGUSTIN DUFLOS, AFTER CLAUDE RONDÉ

^ CROWN OF LOUIS XV

PARIS, 1722
PARTIALLY GILDED SILVER, PASTE IMITATIONS OF THE
ORIGINAL PRECIOUS STONES, EMBROIDERED SATIN
H. 24 CM, DIAM. 22 CM

Used only for their coronations, the personal crowns of the kings of France were kept with other coronation regalia in the royal abbey of Saint-Denis, near Paris. Louis XIV's crown was originally set with 282 diamonds, including the famous 140-carat "Regent," 230 pearls, and 64 colored precious stones, rubies, emeralds, sapphires, and topazes.

FRANÇOIS REGNAULT NITOT (1779-1853)

> NECKLACE AND EARRINGS OF
EMPRESS MARIE-LOUISE

PARIS, 1810
GOLD, DIAMONDS, EMERALDS

After Emperor Napoleon I divorced Joséphine de Beauharnais, the most sumptuous wedding finery was made for his marriage to Marie-Louise, archduchess of Habsburg and daughter of Emperor Francis II in 1810. The most beautiful items were a necklace, diadem, comb, and earrings of diamond and emerald palm leaves.

JACQUES ROETTIERS
> **CENTERPIECE**

PARIS, 1736
CAST AND CHASED SILVER
H. 52 CM, L. 95 CM

A masterpiece of Rococo precious metalwork, created in the refined early-eighteenth-century style that would be displaced by Neoclassicism, this exceptionally large centerpiece was intended to decorate the ceremonial table of the duc de Bourbon. It depicts a stag cornered by hounds. The sides are decorated with wild boars' heads and shells.

⌐ **CABINET**

PARIS, C. 1645
OAK AND POPLAR, EBONY VENEER, DARKENED FRUITWOOD BASE
H. 1.85 M, W. 1.58 M

The Parisian *ébénistes* were named after the wood, *ébène* (ebony), that was used in their furniture. Cabinets such as this one were inspired by Flemish Renaissance cabinets and have extremely refined carved decoration mixing architectural motifs and religious, mythological, and literary themes.

JACOB FRÈRES
> **BED OF MADAME RÉCAMIER**

PARIS, C. 1798
MAHOGANY, GILDED BRONZE, H. 1 M, W. 1.33 M

At the end of the eighteenth century, banker Jacques-Rose Récamier and his wife Juliette had their Parisian town house redesigned by the architect Louis-Martin Berthault. The decor was in what would come to be known as the Empire style. This bed is decorated with swans, palm leaves, and female statuettes.

ANDRÉ-CHARLES BOULLE (1642-1732)
∧ **ARMOIRE**

PARIS, C. 1700
OAK CARCASE, EBONY AND TORTOISESHELL VENEER, BRASS, PEWTER, HORN, AND COLORED WOOD MARQUETRY, GILT-BRONZE MOUNTS, H. 2.65 M, W. 1.35 M

In the extraordinarily sumptuous pieces he produced in his workshop in the Louvre, Boulle elevated the art of marquetry to the highest level of sophistication. Skillfully playing on contrasts between inlaid materials such as tortoiseshell and brass, or daringly combining the most diverse materials, he gave the original forms of his furniture an architectural dimension.

SCULPTURES

ANTOINE-LOUIS BARYE (1795-1875)

LION AND SERPENT

France, 1832-35
Bronze, h. 1.35 m, w. 1.78 m

Both in his realism and his expressiveness, Barye was the incontestable master of that noblest of all subjects in animal sculpture, the king of the animal kingdom subjugating his foes. This dramatic and purposefully terrifying illustration of the forces of nature at work is also a tribute to King Louis-Philippe, who was chosen king of the French during the July Revolution in 1830.

MICHELANGELO BUONARROTI (1475-1564)

< SLAVE

Italy, 1513-15
Marble, h. 2.28 m

Michelangelo never finished his two *Slaves*, which were carved for the monumental tomb of Pope Julius II but not included in the final composition. Their meaning is unclear, but they could depict subjugated passions or the soul chained to the body. The contrast between the finished parts and those still bearing the marks of the sculptor's tools epitomizes art's combat with matter.

When the Musée du Louvre was created in 1793, Michelangelo's *Slaves* were its only examples of "modern" sculpture. The collection grew considerably, however, and in 1824 a gallery was opened displaying a broad range of works from the Renaissance to the nineteenth century, many of which came from the royal palaces and gardens, the former Académie Royale de Peinture et Sculpture, and the Musée des Monuments Français created during the Revolution. Throughout the nineteenth century, the museum acquired the sculptures that today enable us to trace the development of the Neoclassical and Romantic movements. Only later was an attempt made to fill in the gaps in the collection, particularly in medieval sculpture and the foreign schools. The sculpture and objets d'art department split into two in 1892. Subsequent donations and acquisitions have made it the spectacular ensemble it is today. French sculpture is on display in the Richelieu wing and sculpture from other countries in the Denon wing. The former is presented chronologically around two large covered courtyards, ideal settings for the open-air sculpture of the seventeenth, eighteenth, and nineteenth centuries.

As with the Louvre's collection of paintings, which are displayed in separate rooms, the diverse movements of European sculpture are juxtaposed, illustrating the exchanges, influences, and dissemination of styles on a continental scale. The Romanesque period, long neglected, was a time of genuine renewal in sculpture. It rekindled the antique tradition and established original canons linked to its religious subject matter. This was particularly true for architectural decoration, stone capitals, and large Descents from the Cross in wood, both in France and in Italy. The Gothic period in the Île-de-France saw the emergence of a new style of architecture, with cathedrals vying with one another in their daring, and a refined school of sculpture in the service of kings and the Church. The Gothic style continued to develop in the thirteenth, fourteenth, and fifteenth centuries in France, the Germanic countries, and the Netherlands, while Italy began to seek fresh inspiration in antiquity.

During the Quattrocento, the Renaissance revolutionized sculpture and culture, defining new principles. Many artists, such as Michelangelo, the silversmith Cellini, and the architect Bernini, were also sculptors. Their art, which spread throughout Europe, gave man a universal dimension and yielded sublimely beautiful representations of the Greek and Roman myths.

European sculpture in the seventeenth and eighteenth centuries was dominated by Italian Mannerism and then French Classicism, which yielded such spectacular works as the statues of horses for the Château de Marly, Louis XIV's favorite residence.

In the second half of the eighteenth century, Neoclassicism dominated the reception pieces for the royal academy, and permeated the work of Pigalle, Houdon, and Clodion in France and Canova in Italy. It was in the early nineteenth century that the first signs of a reaction against the Neoclassical style manifested themselves in Romantic works that depicted violent emotions with great naturalism.

THE DEAD CHRIST

BURGUNDY, SECOND QUARTER OF THE 12TH CENTURY
MAPLEWOOD, TRACES OF GILDING AND POLYCHROMY
H. 1.55 M, W. 1.68 M

This wooden Christ, characteristic of Romanesque art in Burgundy and similar to the sculptures on the tympanum at Vézelay and the portal at Autun, would have been part of a Descent from the Cross, surrounded by figures. The limp body and refined drapery, originally brightly painted and gilded to enhance their expressive power, have lost nothing of their grace.

∧ HEAD OF EMPRESS ARIADNE

CONSTANTINOPLE OR ROME? EARLY 6TH CENTURY
MARBLE, H. 25.7 CM, W. 22.8 CM

This example of Byzantine art, perpetuating the tradition of the Imperial Roman portrait, has lost nothing of its mystery. The round face crowned by a heavy pearl headdress could be that of Empress Ariadne (474–515), but the stylized features and bulging eyes suggest this was not an attempt at portraiture.

↑ KING CHILDEBERT

ÎLE-DE-FRANCE, C. 1239-1244
STONE WITH TRACES OF POLYCHROMY, H. 1.91 M, W. 0.53 M

This effigy of the Merovingian king Childebert, who died in 558, once greeted the monks at the entrance to the refectory of the abbey his father Clovis founded at Saint-Germain-des-Prés in Paris. The remarkable sophistication of the pose, with the weight slightly on one foot, the naturalism of the detailing, and the grace of the smiling face mark the apogee of monumental Gothic sculpture.

∧ CHARLES V AND JEANNE DE BOURBON

ÎLE-DE-FRANCE, C. 1365-80
STONE, H. 1.95 M, W. 0.71 M AND 0.5 M

These royal effigies once adorned the east entrance to the Louvre, where Charles V, who reigned from 1364 to 1380, had taken up residence. They had a political dimension and were intended to glorify the dynasty. The monarch's realistic face wears a mischievous, almost sardonic expression combined with an air of weariness.

ATTRIBUTED TO ÉVRARD D'ORLÉANS
(KNOWN 1292-1357)

< **ANGEL WITH TWO CRUETS**

ÎLE-DE-FRANCE, C. 1340
MARBLE, H. 52.7 CM, W. 14 CM

This angel holding cruets of eucharistic
wine, symbol of Christ's blood, was
originally part of an altarpiece. It was
commissioned by Queen Jeanne d'Evreux
for the Cistercian abbey of Maubuisson.
The sculptor, who was close to the
court, was also a painter and architect.
This work embodies the elegance and
grace of Gothic sculpture.

TILMAN RIEMENSCHNEIDER
(C. 1460-1531)

> **VIRGIN ANNUNCIATE**

WÜRZBURG, C. 1495
ALABASTER WITH POLYCHROME DECORATION
H. 53 CM, W. 40 CM

The Virgin Mary, full of serenity and dignity,
has stopped reading the Bible to hear from
an angel (which has since disappeared) that
she will give birth to Christ. Originally part of
an altarpiece, this work, with its gentle, delicate features,
undulating hair, and refined drapery, embodies the ideal of
female beauty disseminated by Riemenschneider's studio.
Originally, it would have been painted in bright colors.

ANONYMOUS

∧ **TOMB OF PHILIPPE POT**

BURGUNDY, LAST QUARTER OF THE 15TH CENTURY
PAINTED STONE, H. 1.80 M, W. 2.60 M

The tomb of Philippe (died 1493), seneschal of the duchy
of Burgundy then chamberlain of the king of France, is
exceptional for its composition and illusionistic polychromy.
The recumbent figure is being borne by eight hooded mourners
holding the shields of the eight quarters of his nobility. The
tomb was commissioned by this powerful courtier during
his lifetime for the abbey church of Cîteaux in Burgundy.

GREGOR ERHART (C. 1470-1540)

> **SAINT MARY MAGDALEN**

AUGSBURG, C. 1515-20
POLYCHROMED LIMEWOOD, H. 1.77 M, W. 0.44 M

This penitent Mary Magdalen was originally in a convent
in Augsburg, where she was surrounded by angels. The
feeling of mystical ecstasy exuded by this daringly nude yet
touchingly modest figure satisfied both the Gothic spiritual
tradition and the aesthetic ideals of the Renaissance.

DONATO DI NICCOLO BARDI, KNOWN AS DONATELLO (1386-1466)

< MADONNA AND CHILD

FLORENCE, C. 1440
PAINTED TERRACOTTA RELIEF, H. 1.02 M, W. 0.74 M

One can already see Christ's Passion in the tender face of the Virgin and the anxious expression of the Infant Jesus with his back turned to her. The monumental, geometric composition reflects the Renaissance preoccupation with creating the illusion of spatial depth. The painting and gilding contrast with the flesh tones.

MICHEL COLOMBE (C. 1430-AFTER 1511)

∨ SAINT GEORGE AND THE DRAGON

TOURS, 1508-9
MARBLE ALTARPIECE, H. 1.75 M, W. 2.73 M

Georges d'Amboise, cardinal archbishop of Rouen and minister of Louis XII, commissioned the most famous of late Gothic sculptors to create an altarpiece in the new Italian style for the chapel of his château at Gaillon. This relief, although sometimes clumsy in its transposition of a drawn model, is a blend of medieval fantasy and Renaissance harmony.

BENVENUTO CELLINI (1500-1572)

∨ THE NYMPH OF FONTAINEBLEAU

PARIS, 1542-43
BRONZE, H. 2.05 M, W. 4.09 M

This large tympanum relief, originally sculpted
for an entrance to François I's château at
Fontainebleau, was eventually installed in the
château which Philibert Delorme built for Diane
de Poitiers, Henri II's mistress, at Anet. It was
during his stay in France that the Florentine
sculptor and metalsmith sculpted this hymn to
femininity, whose smooth gentleness contrasts
with the animal furs surrounding her.

JEAN GOUJON (KNOWN 1540-1565)

∧ NYMPH AND SPIRIT

PARIS, C. 1549
STONE, H. 0.73 M, W. 1.95 M

In this fragment from the Fontaine des Innocents,
created to mark King Henri II's ceremonial entry
into Paris, the sensual nymph is indicative of
the spread of the Renaissance into France.
Gujon, who also worked for the king in the
Louvre palace, sculpted antique-style bas-reliefs
with supple, refined, and fluid modeling
emphasized by light drapery.

> SAINT FRANCIS DEAD

SPAIN, MID-17TH CENTURY
WALNUT, GLASS (EYES), BONE (TEETH),
HEMP CORD, H. 87 CM

Legend has it that in 1449 Pope Nicholas V
visited the burial crypt of Saint Francis
of Assisi in the church at Assisi and
the saint's uncorrupted body appeared,
his eyes wide open and the wound
in one of his stigmatized feet still
bleeding. The legend, which became
popular in seventeenth-century Spain,
is realistically depicted here using paint,
glass for the eyes, and bone for the teeth.

PIERRE PUGET (1620-1694)

> MILO OF CROTONA

FRANCE, 1670-82
MARBLE, H. 2.70 M, W. 1.40 M

Milo, hero of his town at the Olympic Games,
wanted to try his strength on a tree but got
his hand trapped and was devoured by wild
beasts. This theme provides a pretext for
a spectacular depiction of pride defeated
by fate and of suffering. A masterpiece of
seventeenth-century sculpture, this work was
given a prominent place in the park at Versailles.

GIANLORENZO BERNINI (1598-1680)

∧ ANGEL WITH THE CROWN OF THORNS

ROME, C. 1667
TERRACOTTA, H. 33 CM, W. 13 CM

Bernini was the foremost architect of
Baroque Rome and also one of its most
prolific sculptors. In charge of celebrations
at the papal court, he planned to decorate
the Ponte Sant'Angelo with colossal statues
of angels meditating on the instruments
of Passion. In this vigorous sketch, the
undulating spiral movement of the drapery
leads up to the face of the angel, which
is roughly modeled.

ADRIAEN DE VRIES (1556-1626)

> MERCURY AND PSYCHE

PRAGUE, 1593
BRONZE, H. 2.15 M, W. 0.92 M

Mercury, winged messenger of the gods,
is departing to take Psyche to Cupid
on Mount Olympus. The lightness
of this bronze group is accentuated
by the spiral composition and the
elongated and fluid contours of the
bodies, influenced by the Mannerist
style that had spread throughout
Europe. De Vries, a Dutchman,
trained in Florence and worked
for the imperial court in Prague.

ANTOINE COYSEVOX (1640-1720)

˅ FAME RIDING PEGASUS

FRANCE, 1699-1702
MARBLE, H. 3.26 M, W. 2.91 M

Fame, commissioned by Louis XIV for the horse pond of his château at Marly, has a pendant, *Mercury*, also riding a winged horse. Epitomizing the official and symbolic art of Louis XIV's reign, the former exalts the king's victories over his enemies, symbolized by the war trophies, while the latter is protecting the arts and commerce once peace has been reestablished.

GUILLAUME I COUSTOU (1677-1746)

˄ DAPHNE CHASED BY APOLLO

FRANCE
MARBLE, H. 1.32, W. 1.35 M

With their sense of movement, these sculptures of running figures, which were reflected in ornamental pools, were intended to bring life to the Classical design of the park at Marly. This group shows the god Apollo pursuing the nymph Daphne, with whom he had fallen in love. Guillaume Coustou, who had already sculpted Hippomenes as a pendant to his Atalante, created it in collaboration with his brother Nicolas.

GUILLAUME I COUSTOU (1677-1746)

> HORSE RESTRAINED BY A GROOM, *ONE OF* THE MARLY HORSES

FRANCE, 1739-45
MARBLE, H. 3.55 M, W. 2.84 M

Coustou was entrusted by Louis XV with the task of replacing his uncle Coysevox's *Fame* and *Mercury*, which had been moved to the Tuileries gardens in Paris. His two *Marly Horses* do away with political rhetoric, paying a striking tribute to untamed nature and manly vigor. This was the century of the Enlightenment, and the grooms symbolize the conquest of the world by human intelligence.

EDME BOUCHARDON (1698-1762)
> CUPID FASHIONING A BOW FROM HERCULES' CLUB
FRANCE, 1747-50
MARBLE, H. 1.73 M, W. 0.75 M

This masterpiece of French Classicism is an ambitious synthesis of the canons of antique sculpture, Italian Mannerism, and direct observation of nature. Indeed, it was criticized for having represented too realistically the adolescent Cupid, whose body forms an elegant spiral as he prepares to unleash another of his formidable arrows.

CLAUDE MICHEL, KNOWN AS CLODION (1738-1814)
∨ LEDA AND THE SWAN
FRANCE, C. 1782
STONE, H. 1.03 M, W. 3.23 M

In Ovid's *Metamorphoses*, Jupiter turns himself into a swan to seduce Leda. She later became a symbol of female sensuality, and it is this aspect that Clodion emphasizes in this relief, accentuating the curves of the bodies, much as Jean Goujon had done during the Renaissance. The work was made for a bathroom designed by the architect Brongniart.

AUGUSTIN PAJOU (1730-1809)
∧ PSYCHE ABANDONED
FRANCE, 1790
MARBLE, H. 1.77 M, W. 0.86 M

Psyche, abandoned by Cupid, whom she had wanted to kill, is an allegory of the suffering of the soul taken from Apuleius' *Golden Ass*. Intended as the pendant to Bouchardon's *Cupid*, this very carnal nude caused a scandal when the plaster model was shown at the 1785 Salon. Even though the tears are timeless, the reference to the live model was considered both too prosaic and immoral.

JEAN-BAPTISTE PIGALLE (1714-1785)

> ## MERCURY ATTACHING HIS WINGED SANDALS

FRANCE, 1753
LEAD, H. 1.87 M, L. 1.08 M

Mercury, god of commerce and messenger of the gods, with his winged sandals and helmet, was the subject for Pigalle's reception piece for the Académie Royale de Peinture et de Sculpture in 1744. Numerous versions were made, including this one in lead, which comes from the Château de Crécy. The work was inspired by the famous *Belvedere Torso* in the Vatican.

ANTOINE-DENIS CHAUDET (1763-1810)

> ## CUPID

FRANCE, 1802-17
MARBLE, H. 77 CM, W. 44 CM

Cupid, portrayed as a charming but mischievous adolescent,
is showing a rose to a butterfly that he is holding by the
wings, a symbol of the torments of the love-stricken soul.
These torments figure on the base, forming part of a fable
about the pains and pleasures of love. The austerity of
Neoclassicism is tempered here by the subtlety
and grace of the forms.

PIERRE JEAN DAVID, KNOWN AS DAVID D'ANGERS (1788-1856)

> PHILOPOEMEN

FRANCE, 1837
MARBLE, H. 2.29 M, W. 0.91 M

This work shows a wounded Achaean drawing a javelin from his leg, a subject taken from Plutarch's *Parallel Lives*. David has given it a universal dimension by exalting the virtue, courage, and grandeur of a hero overcoming pain. Sculpted from life, this nude was commissioned by King Louis-Philippe for the Tuileries.

JEAN-ANTOINE HOUDON (1741-1828)

< LOUISE BRONGNIART AGED FIVE

FRANCE, 1777
TERRACOTTA, H. 34 CM, W. 24 CM

The model for this charming image of childhood was the daughter of the architect Alexandre-Théodore Brongniart (1739–1813), who designed the Bourse de Paris for Napoleon I. Although this antique-style bust is typical of late-eighteenth-century Neoclassicism, its naturalism and presence reflect the Romantic sensibility connected with depictions of the ages of life.

FRANÇOIS RUDE (1784-1855)

^ YOUNG NEAPOLITAN FISHERMAN PLAYING WITH A TURTLE

FRANCE, 1831-33
MARBLE, H. 0.82 M, W. 0.88 M

This work is a remarkable synthesis of the sculptural traditions of classical antiquity, notably the use of the heroic nude and the evocation of mythology, and the Romantic preoccupation with the individual. The fisherman's smile encapsulates the freedom and vivacity of the sculptor's vision, which is both idealized and familiar.

ANTONIO CANOVA (1757-1822)

< PSYCHE REVIVED BY A KISS FROM CUPID

ROME, 1793
MARBLE, H. 1.55 M, W. 1.68 M

The eternal theme of Psyche awakened from eternal sleep by Cupid comes from Apuleius' *Golden Ass*. In this masterpiece of Neoclassical sculpture, Canova treats this allegory in a virtuosic fashion, with a dynamic, pyramidal composition. The delicacy of the embracing bodies is enhanced by the play of light on the marble.

The painting collection is one of the jewels of the Louvre and the reason why it became a museum. During the reign of Louis XVI, the comte d'Angiviller, superintendent of buildings, was charged with creating a "Museum" in the Grande Galerie so that the public could admire the royal collection of paintings. Amassed by successive monarchs since the Renaissance, but principally by François I and Louis XIV, it had until then been housed in various royal residences and in the Garde-Meuble de la Couronne. To fill in the gaps in this collection, which was dominated by the French, Italian, and Flemish schools, Angiviller acquired Dutch, Spanish, and German works. The museum was later enriched with pictures confiscated from emigrating aristocrats and the clergy. It was officially opened to the public in 1793. War booty seized during the Convention and the Empire endowed the Louvre with several of its masterpieces, including Veronese's *Wedding Feast at Cana*,

but most of these treasures were returned to their owners during the Restoration. Throughout the nineteenth and twentieth centuries, the museum endeavored in its acquisitions to respect its original encyclopedic vocation established during the century of the Enlightenment. It also fulfilled its role as custodian of the history of French painting, many of whose nineteenth-century masterpieces are now in the Musée d'Orsay.

Now comprising over eight thousand European paintings ranging in date from the late thirteenth through the nineteenth century, the Department of Paintings has a dual vocation: to preserve and display French painting to the public in the most exhaustive manner possible, and to provide an overview of all European schools, including works by English and Central European artists. The European schools are displayed separately, distributed among the museum's three wings. Their chronological arrangement brings out the close interrelationships between the various schools down the centuries, forging what could be called "European painting," concerning a distinct geographic area that became a reality for painters from the Middle Ages onward.

One has to go back to fourteenth-century Italy, to the humanism advocated by the thinkers of the Renaissance, to find the beginnings of the revolution that took place in European culture. This return to the values of antique art and architecture would for a long time cohabit in Europe with the last manifestations of medieval Gothic art, until the Renaissance finally won the day in the late fifteenth century. Greater realism, due in part to Brunelleschi's discovery of perspective, was now coupled with a new individualist sentiment. The first realistic portraits

began to appear, and also the first works inspired by antiquity, history, and mytho-logy, together with works on religious themes that obeyed the conventions of sacred art. The status and role of the painter evolved. Previously an artisan executing commissions with set subjects, he now became a creator exercising complete freedom of choice over his subject matter and artistic expression. Exceptional figures emerged, such as Leonardo da Vinci, Raphael, and Titian, the friends of princes and theoreticians of their disciplines. Every court in Europe in the sixteenth century endeavored to follow Italy's example in this new vision of art, which would also be influenced by Flemish and Dutch painting. In France,

HIERONYMUS BOSCH (C. 1450-1516)
⌐ **THE SHIP OF FOOLS**
Flanders, c. 1500
Oil on wood, h. 56 cm, w. 32 cm

A bizarre ship flying the flag of the devil, adrift with strange passengers aboard: a nun and a monk drinking together amid a motley crew of miscreants and symbols of lust, desire, stupidity, heresy, madness, and the vices. The painting can be seen as a scathing illustration and condemnation of immorality and folly.

LEONARDO DA VINCI (1452-1519)
< **MONA LISA**
Italy, c. 1503-6
Oil on wood, h. 77 cm, w. 55 cm

This picture, once the jewel of François I's collection and now the most famous painting in the world, continues to fascinate both the public and historians. The enigmatic smile of this beautiful Florentine lady haunts a landscape inspired by the Arno Valley and painted with the *sfumato* technique that Leonardo pioneered. But it is above all the painting's monumentality, imbued with both gravity and gentleness, that is unique.

the influence of Italian artists employed by François I and his successors gave rise to the School of Fontainebleau.

In the early seventeenth century, two trends emerged in parallel: Classicism, whose foundations were laid by the Carracci brothers in Rome, and Caravaggio's naturalistic style using chiaroscuro, which would inspire many artists all over Europe. In the mid-seventeenth century, Rome, now "colonized" by France, saw the end of the supremacy of the Italian school. The emblematic painters of this colony were Nicolas Poussin, Claude Lorraine, and Charles Le Brun, veritable "controller" of the arts during the reign of Louis XIV. Although a trip to Rome remained indispensable for an artist's education, Paris became the cultural capital of Europe. The northern schools, while assimilating the lessons of the Renaissance, developed their own original forms of expression in the sixteenth and seventeenth centuries, giving rise to naturalistic still lifes and genre scenes, as well as the more intimate masterpieces of Rubens, Rembrandt, and Vermeer.

In France, the eighteenth century was dominated by the painters of the Académie Royale de Peinture, whose eclecticism, ranging from Hyacinthe Rigaud's large portraits to Chardin's still lifes, was dominated by what was then considered the noblest of all genres, history painting. But in the middle of the century, painting began gravitating toward Neoclassicism and a return to the virtues of antiquity advocated by the thinkers of the Enlightenment. The emblematic painter of this period was Jacques-Louis David. Elsewhere in Europe, this dominant trend was tempered in the early nineteenth century by the Romantic movement then emerging in England and Germany, epitomized by the work of Turner and Friedrich. They heralded the eclecticism that would give artists greater independence and encourage the experimentation that would later lead to Impressionism and abstraction.

CENNI DI PEPI, KNOWN AS CIMABUE (ACTIVE 1272-1302)

< MAESTÀ (MADONNA AND CHILD ENTHRONED WITH ANGELS)
ITALY, C. 1280
TEMPERA ON WOOD
H. 4.27 M, W. 2.80 M

This monumental *Maestà*, painted for the altar of the church of San Francesco in Assisi, testifies to the culture of Tuscan artists in the late Middle Ages. Although still drawing on the hieratic figurative style derived from Byzantine icons, it displays awareness of the modeling and drapery of antique sculpture, then being rediscovered.

GIOTTO DI BONDONE (C. 1265-1337)

> SAINT FRANCIS OF ASSISI RECEIVING THE STIGMATA
ITALY, C. 1295-1300
TEMPERA ON WOOD, H. 3.13 M, W. 1.63 M

Saint Francis (1182–1226), founder of the mendicant order of the Franciscans, has remained a symbol of Christian spirituality. He is depicted here receiving the stigmata, the marks of the wounds inflicted on Christ during the Passion. The scenes on the predella, the lower part of the altarpiece, illustrate the recognition of the Franciscan order by Pope Innocent III and the saint's familiarity with animals. The figures are set in a spatial depth that anticipates Renaissance art.

GUIDO DI PIETRO, KNOWN AS FRA ANGELICO (KNOWN 1417-1455)

THE CORONATION OF THE VIRGIN

ITALY, C. 1430-32
TEMPERA ON WOOD, H. 2.09 M, W. 2.06 M

The Dominican monk and Florentine painter Fra Angelico used this common theme in medieval art as a pretext for demonstrating some of the new characteristics of Renaissance art: the depiction of figures in space, refined drapery and color (earthly red and heavenly blue), architectural perspective (the tiled floor), and skillful narration in the predella scenes.

ANONYMOUS, MID-14TH CENTURY

< PORTRAIT OF JOHN THE GOOD

FRANCE, C. 1350
WOOD, H. 60 CM, W. 45.5 CM

This portrait, one of the rare easel paintings from the Gothic period to have survived, is also the earliest known French portrait painting. The future king, then duke of Normandy, is realistically portrayed in profile on a gold plain ground, as though on a medal.

ANTONIO PUCCIO, KNOWN AS PISANELLO (C. 1395-1455?)

∨ PORTRAIT OF A YOUNG PRINCESS

ITALY, C. 1440
TEMPERA ON WOOD, H. 43 CM, W. 30 CM

This portrait of a princess of the Este family, who ruled in Ferrara, one of the major centers of the Renaissance, is in the International Gothic style. The rigid, antique-style profile portrait (a convention borrowed from Pisanello's own portrait medals) is softened by the decorative and allegoric richness of the flowers, made up of carnations (symbol of betrothal), columbine (symbol of amorous passion), and juniper (symbol of felicity).

PIERO DELLA FRANCESCA (1416?-1492)

∨ SIGISMONDO PANDOLFO MALATESTA

ITALY, C. 1450-51?
WOOD, H. 44 CM, W. 34 CM

The despotic condottiere of Rimini and humanist patron Sigismondo (1417–68) is still represented in the Gothic manner, in profile, as on a portrait medal, but the naturalism of the bust and modeling of the features were innovations.

JAN VAN EYCK (DIED 1441)
THE MADONNA OF CHANCELLOR ROLIN
FLANDERS, C. 1434
WOOD, H. 66 CM, W. 62 CM

Van Eyck was one of the first painters to use oil-based rather than egg-based paint, and this gave his realistic depictions exceptional definition and finish. Behind the donor facing the Virgin and Child, the landscape dominated by an imaginary town, treated as a picture within the picture, is depicted with incredible precision and its every detail has a symbolic meaning.

ANDREA MANTEGNA (1431-1506)

˅ CRUCIFIXION

ITALY, 1456-59
TEMPERA ON WOOD, H. 76 CM, W. 96 CM

The precocious Mantegna spent the formative years of his life in Padua, the first center of humanism in northern Italy. This work bears the hallmarks of his style, including an archaeological passion for antiquity and a mastery of perspective. The pathetic poses of the tortured bodies and the faces of the mourners add to the painting's power.

PAOLO DI DONO, KNOWN AS PAOLO UCCELLO (1397-1475)

˄ THE BATTLE OF SAN ROMANO

ITALY, C. 1435
TEMPERA ON WOOD, H. 1.82 M, W. 3.17 M

The Medici family commissioned a series of paintings depicting the decisive battle in 1432 between Florence and its rival, Siena. This work is an extraordinarily audacious demonstration of the new science of perspective invented during the Renaissance. The lances, shading of the soldiers' legs, and frozen movements of the horses all enhance the sense of spatial depth and dynamism.

JAIME HUGUET (C. 1415-1492)

˃ THE FLAGELLATION OF CHRIST

SPAIN, C. 1450
WOOD, H. 0.92 M, W. 1.56 M

This panel, created for the front of an altar, was donated to Barcelona Cathedral by the city's shoemakers' guild. It shows the synthesis achieved between the Catalan Gothic style, the discoveries of the Italian Renaissance, and northern European naturalism. The masterly perspective of the architectural space opening onto a landscape is symmetrically organized around the figure of Christ tied to the post.

ENGUERRAND QUARTON (ACTIVE IN PROVENCE 1444-1466)

∧ PIÈTA OF VILLENEUVE-LÈS-AVIGNON

FRANCE, C. 1455
OIL ON WOOD, H. 1.63 M, W. 2.18 M

This work, a scene of mourning, is one of the masterpieces of the Avignon school, which emerged when the papacy was moved to the city in the fourteenth century. In an austere, theatrical composition attenuated by the gentle realism of the faces, Saint John is removing the crown of thorns and Mary Magdalen is drying her tears. On her left, the donor canon seems to be lost in prayer.

ROGIER VAN DER WEYDEN (1399/1400-1464)

↵ THE ANNUNCIATION

FLANDERS, EARLY 14TH CENTURY
WOOD, H. 86 CM, W. 93 CM

Set in an interior that is still medieval, and meticulously painted by one of the most gifted Flemish painters, the Virgin Mary seems to be suffused with light, a sign of the divine destiny being announced to her by the angel Gabriel. The lily and ewer symbolize purity, the extinguished candles announce the advent of divine light, and the richness of the interior reflects the grandeur of Mary's destiny.

JEAN FOUQUET (1420-1478/81)

> PORTRAIT OF CHARLES VII

FRANCE, C. 1445-50
OIL ON WOOD, H. 86 CM, W. 71 CM

This official portrait of the king who defeated the English
with the help of Joan of Arc inaugurated a long tradition.
The bust, treated in a monumental manner, is enhanced by
the splendor of the fabrics and the play of color—green
for hope, red for charity, and white for the fleur-de-lis.
The realism of the face combined with the skillful
composition inspired by Italian Renaissance art reveal
the man himself and glorify his royal power.

JEAN CLOUET (C. 1480-1540/41)

> PORTRAIT OF FRANÇOIS I

FRANCE, C. 1530
WOOD, H. 96 CM, W. 74 CM

In this "icon," inspired by the composition of Fouquet's *Charles VII*,
Clouet left us the finest portrait of the great French Renaissance king
and patron. The realism of the face is enhanced by the richness of
the brocade, the gentle light, and the refined modeling of the hands
in the manner of Leonardo de Vinci and Raphael.

ANTONELLO DA MESSINA (C. 1457-1479)

v PORTRAIT OF A MAN, OR IL CONDOTTIERE

ITALY, 1475
OIL ON WOOD, H. 36 M, W. 30 CM

This portrait, also known as *Il Condottiere*, is a perfect illustration
of the revolution that took place in art during the fifteenth century.
The model is now gazing resolutely at the viewer with expressive
realism. The abandonment of the profile came from Flemish art,
as did the marvelous contrast of light and dark. The figure of
the model is now constructed in space.

ALBRECHT DÜRER (1471-1528)

^ SELF-PORTRAIT

GERMANY, 1493
OIL ON PARCHMENT MOUNTED ON CANVAS
H. 56 CM, W. 44 CM

In his earliest self-portrait, the painter, then aged
twenty-two, depicts himself as a serious young
artist dressed with casual elegance. Brightly lit,
he seems to be facing his destiny, whose key
may lie in the thistle he is holding, a symbol
of marital fidelity or of the Passion of Christ.

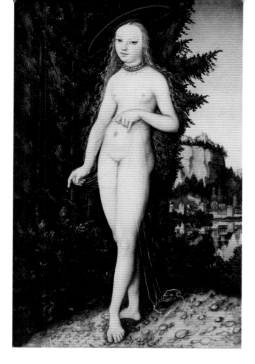

LUCAS CRANACH THE ELDER (1472-1553)

^ VENUS STANDING IN A LANDSCAPE

GERMANY, 1529
OIL ON WOOD, H. 38 CM, W. 25 CM

Cranach, who painted Martin Luther's portrait,
also invented the rather strange genre of the female
nude standing alone in a landscape. The candor and
innocence of her expression combined with her
immodesty give this Gothic Venus a mysterious
and seductive charm, enhanced by the artist's
refined and meticulous technique.

DOMENICO DI TOMMASO BIGORDI,
KNOWN AS GHIRLANDAIO (1449-1494)

< OLD MAN WITH A YOUNG BOY

ITALY, C. 1490
OIL ON WOOD, H. 63 CM, W. 46 CM

A poignant testament to the vogue for portraiture in Florence,
this double portrait was inspired by the delicate precision of
Flemish painting. It is an allegory of the ravages of time and
the timelessness of family tenderness. The almost hyperrealist
landscape outside, a picture within the picture, gives depth
to this otherwise tightly framed close-up composition.

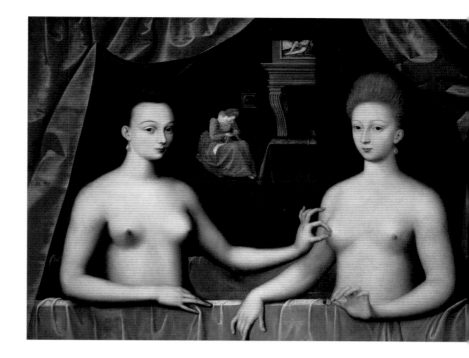

SCHOOL OF FONTAINEBLEAU, LATE 16TH CENTURY

^ GABRIELLE D'ESTRÉES AND ONE OF HER SISTERS

FRANCE, C. 1594
OIL ON WOOD, H. 96 CM, W. 1.25 M

The painter is inviting us into a world of intimacy and allegory.
The gesture made by the sister of the beautiful Gabrielle is
a reference to the child that Henri IV's mistress will soon
bear him, as is the busy wet nurse in the background. The
theme of the bath provides a pretext for the sensual depiction
of the two women, which is accentuated by the folds of the
red curtain that has been drawn to reveal the scene.

ALESSANDRO FILIPEPI, KNOWN AS BOTTICELLI
(C. 1445-1510)

> VENUS AND THE THREE GRACES PRESENTING GIFTS TO A YOUNG WOMAN

ITALY, C. 1483
FRESCO, H. 2.12 M, W. 2.64 M

This fresco, originally part of the decoration
of a villa, demonstrates the erudition of
the painter and his client, who were both
familiar with Neoplatonism. It is an allegory
of the gifts given by the gods to mortals
to give them "ideal beauty," which is
expressed here by the gentleness of
the lines and lightness of the colors.

HANS MEMLING (C. 1435-1494)

> ## THE VIRGIN AND CHILD BETWEEN SAINT JAMES AND SAINT DOMINIC

FLANDERS, C. 1489-90
OIL ON WOOD
H. 1.30 M, W. 1.60 M

This picture is a memorial to a family decimated by the plague in 1489. Jan Floreins, a rich spice merchant in Bruges, accompanied by his son, is being presented to the Virgin by his patron saint. His wife and daughters are being presented by the saint who founded the order into which the widow would retire. This devotional work is a marvelous synthesis of precision and emotional force.

LEONARDO DA VINCI (1452-1519)

> ## THE VIRGIN AND CHILD WITH SAINT ANNE

ITALY, C. 1510
OIL ON WOOD, H. 1.68 M, W. 1.30 M

This painting reveals Leonardo's fascination with the effects of atmosphere on color. The gradation of bluish tones in the background creates a setting of intense depth for the scene, whose protagonists form a dynamic pyramid, an entirely new treatment of the theme.

RAFFAELLO SANTI, KNOWN AS RAPHAEL (1483-1520)

< ## VIRGIN AND CHILD WITH SAINT JOHN THE BAPTIST, *KNOWN AS* LA BELLE JARDINIÈRE

ITALY, 1508
OIL ON WOOD, H. 1.22 M, W. 0.80 M

In this picture, whose clear, geometric composition and grading of tones for the landscape are reminiscent of Leonardo, Raphael conveys all the tenderness, serenity, and intimacy of this scene of the Virgin Mary holding the Infant Jesus, watched by the young John the Baptist. With its balanced design, the painting encapsulates the ideals of the High Renaissance.

AGNOLO DI COSIMO DI MARIANO TORI,
KNOWN AS BRONZINO (1503-1572)

⌐ **PORTRAIT OF A MAN HOLDING
A STATUETTE**

ITALY, C. 1550
OIL ON CANVAS, H. 99 CM, W. 79 CM

It was thought for a long time that this portrait,
bought by Louis XIV in 1671, was of a young sculptor,
but he is now believed to be a young patrician.
The statuette of Fame he is delicately holding
symbolizes his aspirations. The refinement of the muted
colors, the restricted space, rich detail, and frankness
of the subject's gaze combine to strange effect.

ANDREA D'AGNOLO DI FRANCESCO,
KNOWN AS ANDREA DEL SARTO (1486-1530)

> **CHARITY**

ITALY, 1518
OIL ON CANVAS, H. 1.85 M, W. 1.37 M

That prime Christian virtue, Charity,
is shown here with her attributes:
the three children she is taking care
of, and the vase and pomegranate at
her feet. A major work of the late
Florentine Renaissance, with its
classical composition and balanced
forms, it was commissioned by François I,
who had invited the artist to France.

GIOVANNI BATTISTA DI JACOPO, KNOWN AS ROSSO FIORENTINO (1496-1540)

↵ **PIETÀ**

ITALY, C. 1530-35
OIL ON WOOD MOUNTED ON CANVAS, H. 1.27 M, W. 1.63 M

This work by the red-haired Florentine artist, painted during his stay
at Fontainebleau, testifies to the spread of Mannerism into France.
The dramatic intensity of this scene of the Virgin Mary, John, and Mary
Magdalen mourning Christ is reinforced by the theatrical framing,
cramped composition, expressive gestures, and vivid colors.

JACOPO CARRUCCI, KNOWN AS IL PONTORMO (1494-1556)

> **MADONNA AND CHILD WITH SAINT ANNE
AND FOUR SAINTS**

ITALY, 1527-29
OIL ON WOOD, H. 2.28 M, W. 1.76 M

This *pala* (large altarpiece) commemorates the expulsion of a tyrant
from Florence in the fourteenth century. Saint Anne, patron saint
of Florence, is accompanied by Saint Benedict, Saint Sebastian,
Saint Peter, and the Good Thief. The languid, swirling forms, acidic
colors, and dark background are all characteristic of Mannerism.

PAOLO CALIARI, KNOWN AS VERONESE (1528-1588)

THE MARRIAGE AT CANA

ITALY, 1562-63
OIL ON CANVAS
H. 6.66 M, W. 9.90 M

This painting, brought back to France
by Napoleon Bonaparte in 1798, came from
San Giorgio Maggiore in Venice, designed by
Palladio. The theme chosen by the Benedictine
monks was that of Christ's first miracle,
which took place during a wedding feast
at Cana in Galilee. The married couple,
with their sumptuous Renaissance clothes,
are banished to the end of the table, while
Christ, his mother, and the apostles, with
their humble antique garb, occupy the center
of the scene. Using a small range of colors,
the artist has nonetheless succeeded in
conveying the full magnificence of the feast.

HANS HOLBEIN (1497/98-1543)

∧ ERASMUS

GERMANY, 1523
OIL ON WOOD, H. 42 CM, W. 32 CM

Erasmus (1469–1536) was one of the major humanist thinkers of the Renaissance. Holbein portrays the great Dutch scholar writing his commentary on the Gospel of Saint Mark in *Paraphrases in Novum Testamentum* in profile, in keeping with the tradition of the antique portrait medal. He has a grave expression and is dressed in plain clothes. This sensitive portrait seeks above all to express the subject's personality.

PIETER BRUEGHEL THE ELDER (C. 1525-1569)

∧ THE BEGGARS

FLANDERS, 1568
OIL ON WOOD, H. 18 CM, W. 21.5 CM

The monumentality and masterful composition of this tiny painting are a testament to Brueghel's genius. Is this picture of beggars—five men and a woman—a satire of human misery or an allusion to the carnival of beggars aping different classes of society? The meaning of this work remains a mystery.

HANS BALDUNG GRIEN (1484/85-1545)

> THE KNIGHT, THE YOUNG GIRL, AND DEATH

GERMANY
OIL ON WOOD, H. 35 CM, W. 30 CM

This strange composition by one of Dürer's pupils is an allegory of love triumphing over death, an eternal theme which here expresses a certain optimism in the face of fate. The expressionist feel of the skeleton, which could have come straight out of a dance of death, contrasts with the lively and colorful figures of the embracing couple.

QUENTIN MASSYS (1465/66-1530)

˅ THE MONEYLENDER AND HIS WIFE

HOLLAND, 1514
OIL ON WOOD, H. 70 CM, W. 67 CM

"Use honest scales and honest weights" is the moral of this scene
of a moneylender keeping his accounts, inspired by a lost work by
van Eyck. The naturalistic details combine to create a solemn and
symbolic "still life," in which the open book with an illumination
of the Virgin Mary recalls the spiritual dimension of existence.

ANTONIO ALLEGRI, KNOWN AS CORREGGIO (C. 1489-1534)

^ THE MYSTIC MARRIAGE OF SAINT CATHERINE

ITALY, C. 1526-27
OIL ON WOOD, H. 1.05 M, W. 1.02 M

In the delicate harmony of this scene, Correggio achieves
a successful synthesis of the refined art of Leonardo and Raphael
and Venetian spontaneity of color. Catherine is symbolically
united with the Infant Jesus, while in the background we see
her terrible martyrdom after refusing to give up her faith
and marry the Emperor Maxentius.

JACOPO ROBUSTI, KNOWN AS TINTORETTO
(1518-1594)

< SUSANNA AT HER BATH

ITALY, BETWEEN 1550 AND 1560
OIL ON CANVAS, H. 1.67 M, W. 2.38 M

The biblical story of Susanna was a moral
subject par excellence. She was lusted
after by two elderly lechers, but when
she spurned them, they accused her of
committing adultery with a young man.
The story provides Tintoretto with a
chance to celebrate the female nude.
The contrast between the voyeurs and
the intimate scene in the foreground is
accentuated by the use of color and light
to heighten the sensuality of Susanna.

TIZIANO VECELLIO, KNOWN AS TITIAN
(1488/1490-1576)

< CONCERT CHAMPÊTRE

ITALY, C. 1510
OIL ON CANVAS, H. 1.05 M, W. 3.65 M

This "concert" is a friendly contest between
the music of the town and the country,
represented by the two men accompanied
by their muses. The scene is set in Arcadia,
the Grecian mythical paradise that inspired
the Renaissance poets. Line and color
combine to create a balanced harmony.

PIETRO DI CRISTOFORO VANNUCCI, KNOWN AS PERUGINO (C. 1448-1523)

^ APOLLO AND MARSYAS

ITALY, C. 1495
OIL ON WOOD, H. 39 CM, W. 29 CM

The theme of this painting, frequently treated in the sculpture of antiquity,
is taken from Ovid's *Metamorphoses*. The painting shows the flute playing
contest between the young Silenus Marsyas and Apollo, god of beauty and
the arts, judged by the Muses. Marsyas lost and was flayed alive, but instead
of showing this, Perugino preferred this peaceful and suggestive confrontation
full of poetic allusions to further assert painting's superiority over sculpture.

DOMENIKOS THEOTOKOPOULOS,
KNOWN AS EL GRECO (1541-1614)

> ### CHRIST ON THE CROSS ADORED BY TWO DONORS

SPAIN, C. 1585-90
OIL ON CANVAS, H. 2.60 M, W. 1.71 M

The Cretan-born painter El Greco forged his own original and timeless expressionistic style. In this work, there is no superfluous landscape to distract us. The viewer's attention is entirely focused on the tormented figure of Christ, which is echoed by the lugubrious and menacing sky in which light and darkness, the sacred and the profane, battle with one another.

GERRIT VAN HONTHORST (1590-1656)

v ### CONCERT ON A BALCONY

HOLLAND, 1624
OIL ON CANVAS, H. 1.68 M, W. 1.78 M

Honthorst epitomizes the stylistic exchanges that took place in European painting in the early seventeenth century. Inspired during his stay in Italy as much by the Carracci brothers' classicism as Caravaggio's realism, he combined the light figures of the angels and his very real Dutch musicians in a trompe-l'oeil setting whose theatricality is accentuated by the drapery.

MICHELANGELO MERISI, KNOWN AS CARAVAGGIO (1571-1610)

> ### THE DEATH OF THE VIRGIN

ITALY, C. 1601-5/6
OIL ON CANVAS, H. 3.69 M, W. 2.45 M

Commissioned for a convent, this work was rejected by the clergy. Caravaggio had deliberately given the figures in his painting—the dead Virgin Mary surrounded by the apostles and Mary Magdalen—a human dimension that differed markedly from the usual representations found in religious works. He made darkness the dominant element to highlight the colors and provide a contrast with the light. Caravaggio revolutionized painting at the turn of the seventeenth century.

CLAUDE VIGNON (1593-1670)

> ### THE YOUNG SINGER

FRANCE, C. 1622-23
OIL ON CANVAS, H. 95 CM, W. 90 CM

The stark realism and fantastic chiaroscuro introduced by Caravaggio were highly influential, spreading to France and the rest of Europe. Artists began to depict scenes from daily life, such as this one showing an elegantly dressed young man painted with very free brushwork.

SIMON VOUET (1590-1649)

∨ WEALTH

FRANCE, C. 1640
OIL ON CANVAS, H. 1.70 M, W. 1.24 M

Vouet, whose early works had been influenced by
Caravaggio, infused French painting with brilliant color.
In this allegory painted for Louis XIII, Wealth, with
an ample movement of her golden drapery, is turning
her back on Reason to give in to Temptation. The
contrast between the yellow and pinkish tones
illuminates the drapery.

GUIDO RENI (1575-1642)

∧ DEIANEIRA AND THE CENTAUR NESSUS

ITALY, 1617-21
OIL ON CANVAS, H. 2.39 M, W. 1.93 M

The composition is the most important element in this work, which was
commissioned by Ferdinando di Gonzaga for the Villa Favorita in Mantua.
Renaissance order and poise have given way here to the sinuous lines of
Mannerism and the classicism of the flamboyant drapery, which give this scene
from Ovid's *Metamorphoses* its extraordinary dramatic energy. On the right,
we see Hercules about to come and save his wife from the centaur.

ANNIBALE CARRACCI (1560-1609)

< HUNTING *AND* FISHING

ITALY, C. 1585-88
OIL ON CANVAS, H. 1.36 M, W. 2.53 M

The academy opened by the brothers Annibale and Agostino Carracci in
Bologna in 1585 became the center for a new form of classicism opposed
to Caravaggio's verism. These two visions of country life illustrate the synthesis
they achieved between the characteristics of the great Renaissance masters
and close observation of nature.

GIUSEPPE ARCIMBOLDO (C. 1527-1593)

^ AUTUMN

ITALY, C. 1573
OIL ON CANVAS, H. 76 CM, W. 63 CM

In 1573 Emperor Maximilian II of Habsburg commissioned the Milanese artist Arcimboldo to paint a series of four pictures illustrating the seasons, to be offered to the Elector Augustus of Saxony. Each of these four allegorical profiles is composed of the fruits of each season. The virtuoso technique of this Mannerist artist gives them a fantastical and ambiguous appearance.

DOMENICO ZAMPIERI,
KNOWN AS DOMENICHINO (1581-1641)

> SAINT CECILIA WITH AN ANGEL HOLDING A SCORE

ITALY, C. 1617
OIL ON CANVAS, H. 1.60 M, W. 1.20 M

The patron saint of musicians, whose body was found in Rome in 1599, is the pretext here for an elegantly composed female portrait. A work of intimate devotion—one can even read the score the angel is holding— this painting illustrates the renewal in the worship of saints encouraged by the Counter-Reformation as an antidote to the austerity of Protestantism.

FRANCISCO DE ZURBARÁN (1598-1664)

> SAINT BONAVENTURE'S BODY LYING IN STATE

SPAIN, 1629
OIL ON CANVAS, H. 2.45 M, W. 2.20 M

The white diagonal formed by the body of the reformer of the Franciscan Order in Andalusia is suffused with a mysterious and dramatic light contrasting with the cadaverous blackness of his face. In the same way, the gray monochrome of the monks' robes contrasts with the refined fabric of the catafalque and the garments of Pope Gregory X and the King of Aragon.

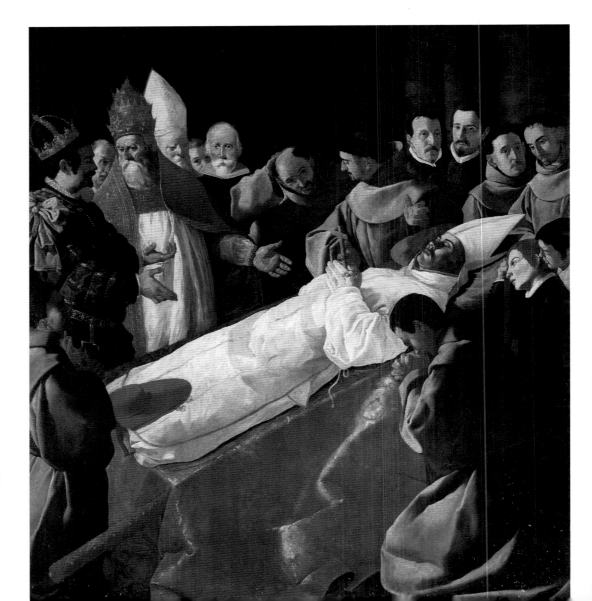

JUSEPE DE RIBERA (1591-1652)

˅ THE CLUBFOOTED BOY

SPAIN, 1642
OIL ON CANVAS, H. 1.64 M, W. 0.94 M

"Give me alms for the love of god" is the message this young clubfooted beggar is proudly displaying. Ribera captures the human condition with great realism and humanity in this painting. The innocence of his toothless smile and the candid gaze illuminate this monumental composition. This depiction of a request for charity casts the Spanish Golden Age in a less flattering light.

BARTOLOMÉ ESTEBAN MURILLO (1618-1682)

˅ THE YOUNG BEGGAR

SPAIN, C. 1650
OIL ON CANVAS, H. 1.34 M, W. 1 M

Inspired by Caravaggio, Murillo gives us a striking vision of childhood full of compassion and poetic realism. A young boy dressed in rags, sitting amid the crumbs of a frugal meal, is delousing himself as he warms himself in the shaft of sunlight starkly illuminating the dark corner in which he is hiding his misery.

JOHANNES VERMEER (1632-1675)

> THE ASTRONOMER

HOLLAND, 1668
OIL ON CANVAS, H. 50 CM, W. 45 CM

This is one of the finest depictions of the scientist-philosopher absorbed in contemplation of the celestial globe. The small scale, rich detail, and warm light invite the viewer to join him in his studious and meditative contemplation.

GEORGES DE LA TOUR (1593-1652)

∨ THE CHEAT WITH THE ACE OF DIAMONDS

FRANCE, C. 1635
OIL ON CANVAS, H. 1.06 M, W. 1.46 M

De La Tour is illustrating here the classical theme of innocence and virtue confronting vice and debauchery. The young man on the right is exposed to the dual temptation of the flesh and gambling, and in either case he will lose his gold. The perverse exchange of gestures and looks reveals the complicity between the cheat and the two women. Following in the footsteps of Caravaggio, de La Tour displays extraordinary mastery of chiaroscuro and texture.

JOHANNES VERMEER (1632-1675)

> THE LACEMAKER

HOLLAND, C. 1665-75
OIL ON WOOD, H. 24 CM, W. 21 CM

In the composition of this small painting, Vermeer exploited optical artifices, notably the enlarged and unfocused foreground and the neutral background, to draw the viewer's gaze to the precise gesture of the girl absorbed in her task. The atmosphere of tranquillity that imbues this silent, intimate scene is evoked with great delicacy.

LOUIS (OR ANTOINE) LE NAIN (C. 1600/10-1648)

> THE PEASANT FAMILY

FRANCE, C. 1630
OIL ON CANVAS, H. 1.13 M, W. 1.59 M

The Le Nain brothers specialized in scenes from peasant life, and this one is remarkable for the nobility of its poses and its serenity. Unlike their contemporaries, they favored a limited palette of muted colors, and their classical approach to composition differed from that of Flemish and Dutch genre paintings.

REMBRANDT HARMENSZ. VAN RIJN (1606-1669)

< **BATHSHEBA**

HOLLAND, 1654
OIL ON CANVAS, H. 1.42 M, W. 1.42 M

Bathsheba, desired by King David, is meditating on the fate the letter has just revealed to her. The model for this dramatic nude, almost Venetian in its hues and sensuality, was the painter's companion, Hendrickje Stoffels. The picture symbolizes in an allegorical manner a woman's dignity in submitting to a man's desire. The intimate tenderness of the scene is accentuated by the rich textures.

FRANS HALS (C. 1581/85-1666)

< **THE GYPSY GIRL**

HOLLAND, C. 1628-30
OIL ON WOOD, H. 58 CM, W. 52 CM

The title of this key work is misleading, as it is almost certainly a portrait of a prostitute. Although it is an allegoric genre painting, Hals has imbued it with a realism inspired by Caravaggio. The variation in brushwork, from delicate strokes to quick, loose ones, brings out all the dynamism of this popular figure symbolizing female sensuality.

PIETER DE HOOCH (1629-1684)

∨ **YOUNG WOMAN DRINKING**

HOLLAND, 1658
OIL ON CANVAS, H. 69 CM, W. 60 CM

Pieter de Hooch, Vermeer's precursor in Delft, has frozen the figures in this painstakingly architectural composition so as not to disturb the luminous harmony of its perspective. This is in fact a moral allegory: a prostitute, a procuress, and two clients are drinking, while the picture of Christ and the adulteress on the wall on the right announces their fate.

GERRIT DOU (1613-1675)

∨ **THE DROPSICAL WOMAN**

HOLLAND, 1663
OIL ON WOOD, H. 83 CM, W. 67 CM

The medical consultation, a "vanitas" illustrating human fragility, was a frequent subject of genre painting, but it is this picture's extraordinary treatment which makes it so unique. The illusionistic effects, meticulous technique, minute detail, and variety of expressions are all hallmarks of this prodigious painter.

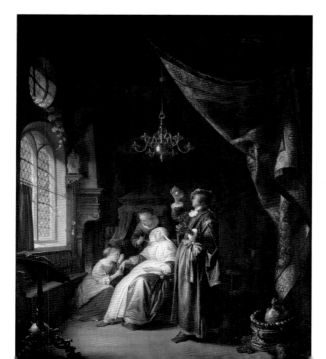

CLAUDE GELLÉE, KNOWN AS CLAUDE LORRAIN (1602-1682)

∧ SEAPORT AT SUNSET

FRANCE, 1639
OIL ON CANVAS, H. 1.03 M, W. 1.37 M

As Roman as Nicolas Poussin, Claude Lorrain sought inspiration in antique and modern Rome for his imaginary and idealized landscapes of architecture bathed in light, often given a historic or mythological pretext. The classical composition is accentuated by the perspective, which converges here on the setting sun in a gradation of warm hues.

JACOB VAN RUISDAEL (C. 1628/29-1682)

< THE RAY OF SUNLIGHT

HOLLAND, C. 1665-70
OIL ON CANVAS, H. 83 CM, W. 99 CM

Works such as this one, "a vast stretch of countryside lit by a ray of sunlight," with picturesque ruins and tiny figures beneath a huge, dramatic sky, established Ruisdael as the greatest Dutch landscape painter. The yellow of the starkly lit cornfield contrasts with the delicate palette elsewhere to create a sense of the sublime.

EUSTACHE LE SUEUR (1616-1655)

> ## CLIO, EUTERPE, AND THALIA

FRANCE, C. 1652
OIL ON WOOD, H. 1.3 M, W. 1.3 M

This fragment from the decor of the mansion of President Lambert is
an example of the sumptuous decoration of Parisian residences in the
seventeenth century. Part of a "concert of the nine muses," it depicts
the muses of history, music, and drama. The elegant figures, refined
colors, and balanced composition typify Le Sueur's classical style.

NICOLAS POUSSIN (1594-1665)

∨ ## THE ARCADIAN SHEPHERDS

FRANCE, C. 1638-40
OIL ON CANVAS, H. 0.85 M, W. 1.21 M

This meditation on death inspired by the antique ideal is one of
the masterpieces of the Louvre's collection of over forty pictures
by the most Italian of all French painters, Nicolas Poussin. The idyllic
landscape backdrop for this scene dominated by the blue of wisdom
and the yellow of intelligence gives this vision of Greek mythology
a poetic dimension.

CHARLES LE BRUN (1619-1690)

> ## CHANCELLOR SÉGUIER

FRANCE, C. 1657-61
OIL ON CANVAS, H. 2.95 M, W. 3.57 M

Everything about this equestrian portrait celebrates
the elevated rank of Chancellor Séguier, the most
important person in the kingdom after the king. Gold
and silver dominate this work by Louis XIV's First Painter,
whose pyramidal composition is enlivened by the circle
of young pages escorting the horse.

HYACINTHE RIGAUD (1659-1743)

> ## LOUIS XIV

FRANCE, 1701
OIL ON CANVAS, H. 2.77 M, W. 1.94 M

The Sun King, symbol of absolute monarchy, commissioned
this portrait when he was sixty-three as a gift to his grandson
Philip V of Spain, but changed his mind and kept the original
at Versailles. All the symbols of royal power are present in
this archetypal official portrait: the crown and the hand of
justice on a cushion, the ermine-lined fleur-de-lis coronation
mantle, the sword of Charlemagne, and the scepter of Henri IV.

PETER PAUL RUBENS (1577-1640)

∨ ## THE ARRIVAL OF MARIE DE MÉDICIS
AT MARSEILLE

HOLLAND, BETWEEN 1621 AND 1625
OIL ON CANVAS, H. 3.94 M, W. 2.95 M

This heroic apparition is one of the twenty-four large
paintings retracing the life of Henri IV's wife that Rubens
painted for the Médicis gallery in the Luxembourg Palace. In
this masterpiece of Baroque art, realism and the fantastic blend
in a dynamic, swirling composition bathed in an unreal light.

ANTHONY VAN DYCK (1599-1641)

∧ ## CHARLES I, KING OF ENGLAND,
AT THE HUNT

HOLLAND, C. 1635
OIL ON CANVAS, H. 2.66 M, W. 2.07 M

This majestic yet intimate portrait of Charles I
of England (1600–1649) illustrates his elegance in all
circumstances. Despite the portrait's apparent realism,
this is a portrayal of a king in all his majesty, enhanced
by the horse, inspired by antiquity and Titian, and
also by the rich color harmonies and textures.

JEAN-SIMÉON CHARDIN (1699-1779)

< **THE SKATE**

FRANCE, 1728
OIL ON CANVAS, H. 1.14 M, W. 1.46 M

In 1728, Chardin, a painter of still lifes, a genre considered inferior to history painting, was admitted to the Académie Royale de Peinture et de Sculpture on the strength of this brilliant demonstration of illusionistic skill, the equal of the Flemish works then immensely popular in France. Diderot wrote about this picture, the "magic" of whose colors he praised, that "the object is disgusting; but it is the fish's very flesh, its skin, its blood."

JEAN-SIMÉON CHARDIN (1699-1779)

∨ **SAYING GRACE**

FRANCE, 1740
OIL ON CANVAS, H. 49.5 CM, W. 38.5 CM

"Here is the real painter; here is the true colorist," Diderot exclaimed before Chardin's works. A painter of intimate subjects, he gave genre scenes and still lifes a new dimension with his vigorous brushwork and the tender attention he paid to his subjects, whether children, fruit, or a skate coveted by a cat.

FRANÇOIS BOUCHER (1703-1770)

∧ **MORNING COFFEE**

FRANCE, 1739
OIL ON CANVAS, H. 81.5 CM, W. 65.5 CM

Diderot adored Chardin's truthfulness and detested the "tastefulness" of Boucher's mythological visions of chubby cherubs. The family depicted in this rare genre scene in the Dutch manner could well be the painter's. They are drinking coffee in a refined and typically eighteenth-century interior decorated in the Rococo style.

JEAN-ANTOINE WATTEAU (1684-1721)

> **PIERROT,** *ALSO KNOWN AS* **GILLES**

FRANCE, C. 1718-19
OIL ON CANVAS, H. 1.84 M, W. 1.49 M

This unusual full-length portrait of a commedia dell'arte character may have been painted as a sign for a cabaret opened in Paris by a friend of the painter. This dreamy Pierrot, appearing on a makeshift rural stage surrounded by other actors, is painted on a monumental scale and captivates with his melancholic expression and gaze.

JEAN-HONORÉ FRAGONARD (1732-1806)

v THE BOLT

FRANCE, C. 1777
OIL ON CANVAS, H. 73 CM, W. 93 CM

This work, which became the symbol of eighteenth-century libertine painting, is also a demonstration of virtuosity on the artist's part. A long diagonal traverses the painting from apple to bolt, from temptation to fall, leading through the temptations of the flesh passionately enacted by the two lovers.

↗ THE SON PUNISHED

FRANCE, 1778
OIL ON CANVAS, H. 1.30 M, W. 1.62 M

This is the second part of a family drama in two acts: the son enlists in the army and abandons the family he is supporting; when he returns, he finds his father dead of despair. This genre painting in the antique-style inspiring and promoting domestic virtues exemplified what Diderot called the "morality in painting" that could counter "debauchery and vice."

HUBERT ROBERT (1733-1808)

> ## THE PONT DU GARD

FRANCE, 1787
OIL ON CANVAS, H. 2.42 M, W. 2.42 M

This view of a Roman aqueduct was part of a series Robert, also a landscape gardener, was commissioned to paint for Louis XVI's apartments. Other works in the series included the antique monuments at Nîmes and Orange. This period was marked by a return to antique sources and scenes of ruins like this one became a form of "vanitas."

THOMAS GAINSBOROUGH (1727-1788)

> CONVERSATION IN A PARK

ENGLAND, C. 1746-47
OIL ON CANVAS, H. 73 CM, W. 68 CM

In this "conversation piece," a genre popular
in eighteenth-century England, the young painter
has portrayed himself with Margaret, whom he
married in 1746. The young couple seem to be
inviting the viewer to share this intimate moment
in an English garden with a temple-like folly in the
background. Their refined clothes offer a delicate
interplay of pastel shades and vivid colors.

JOSHUA REYNOLDS (1723-1792)

< MASTER HARE

ENGLAND, C. 1788-89
OIL ON CANVAS, H. 77 CM, W. 63 CM

Thanks to this portrait painted when he was two years
old, Francis John Hare became a symbol of the attachment
to childhood that became a hallmark of English Romanticism.
With his warm, luminous palette inspired by Titian,
Joshua Reynolds creates a symbiosis between subject
and surrounding landscape in this delicate evocation of
the age of innocence.

FRANCISCO JOSÉ DE GOYA Y LUCIENTES (1746-1828)

> THE MARQUESA DE LA SOLANA

SPAIN, C. 1795
OIL ON CANVAS, H. 1.81 M, W. 1.22 M

The official portraitist of the Madrid aristocracy, Goya captured
the personalities of his subjects through a combination of
illusionistic realism and an evocative quality that anticipated
Impressionism. The Marquesa de la Solana, an erudite and
charitable young woman already suffering from a fatal illness,
died shortly after this grave and refined portrait was painted.

JACQUES-LOUIS DAVID (1748-1825)

˅ THE OATH OF THE HORATII

FRANCE, 1784
OIL ON CANVAS, H. 3.30 M, W. 4.25 M

As soon as this depiction of the courage of the Roman Horatii against the Curiatii
of Alba was shown at the 1785 Salon it became the manifesto of the emerging
Neoclassical school of painting and established David as its undisputed leader.
The austere decor inspired by the Greek Doric style divides the composition
and contrasts with the movements of the virile men and despairing women.

ANNE-LOUIS GIRODET DE ROUSSY-TRIOSON
(1767-1824)

> THE BURIAL OF ATALA

FRANCE, 1808
OIL ON CANVAS, H. 2.07 M, W. 2.67 M

This Romantic painting inspired by a novel
by Chateaubriand eloquently illustrates
the sensibility that pervaded art in
France in the early nineteenth century.
It also bears witness to the revival
of Christianity after the Revolution.
"Indian" exoticism and "national" piety
are brought together here in the manner
of a Greek tragedy.

PIERRE NARCISSE GUÉRIN (1774-1833)

> THE RETURN OF
MARCUS SEXTUS

FRANCE, 1799
OIL ON CANVAS, H. 2.17 M, W. 2.43 M

This fictitious scene shows Marcus Sextus,
who has was banished by Sulla, having
returned home to find his daughter
weeping at his dead wife's bedside. It
was interpreted as an allegory of the
return of émigrés who had fled France
during the Revolution. The picture's
emotional intensity makes it one of
the most moving examples of the
austere yet tender Necoclassicism
of this refined disciple of David.

MARIE-GUILLEMINE BENOIST (1768-1826)

∧ PORTRAIT OF A NEGRESS
FRANCE, 1800
OIL ON CANVAS, H. 81 CM, W. 65 CM

Marie-Guillemine Benoist, who
worked in David's studio, is one
of the few woman artists to have
works in the Louvre. This portrait
of a West Indian servant has great
majesty and sobriety. The coldness
and austerity of Neoclassicism is here
softened by a feminine sensibility.

ÉLISABETH-LOUISE VIGÉE-LE BRUN (1755-1842)

∨ MADAME VIGÉE-LE BRUN AND HER DAUGHTER
FRANCE, 1789
OIL ON WOOD, H. 1.30 M, W. 0.94 M

Vigée-Le Brun, the most famous woman painter of her time,
was offical painter to Marie-Antoinette and the darling of European
courts as far afield as Russia. Like this simple image of maternal
love, her intimate portraits of her contemporaries are graceful
and delicately executed.

ANTOINE-JEAN GROS (1771-1835)

> NAPOLEON VISITING THE
PESTHOUSE AT JAFFA
FRANCE, 1804
OIL ON CANVAS, H. 5.23 M, W. 7.15 M

Gros used this episode in Napoleon's
Syrian campaign in 1799 to create
a work of propaganda in which
the emperor displays his heroism
by visiting plague-stricken soldiers.
Gros was one of the first painters to
paint Orientalist paintings, although
he himself never visited the Near East.
The Eastern architecture has been
painted with meticulous care, and
the expressive faces add to the
impact of the work.

PIERRE PAUL PRUD'HON (1758-1823)

> ## THE EMPRESS JOSEPHINE

FRANCE, 1805
OIL ON CANVAS, H. 2.44 M, W. 1.79 M

The melancholic figure of the woman
Napoleon repudiated in 1809 because she
could not bear him an heir is portrayed
in the solitude of the grounds of her
château at Malmaison. The picture,
typical of the eclectic spirit of the time,
is composed in the manner of eighteenth-
century English portraits and suffused
with a soft light reminiscent of Italian
Renaissance painting.

JACQUES-LOUIS DAVID (1748-1825)

THE CORONATION OF THE EMPEROR NAPOLEON I AND THE CROWNING OF THE EMPRESS JOSÉPHINE

FRANCE, 1806-8
OIL ON CANVAS, H. 6.21 M, W. 9.79 M

On December 2, 1804, in Notre-Dame Cathedral in Paris, Napoleon Bonaparte was crowned emperor in the presence of Pope Pius VII. David was asked to commemorate the event. He chose to depict the moment when the emperor crowned the empress Joséphine. In this extraordinarily detailed but historically inaccurate re-creation of the ceremony, David assembled a spectacular portrait gallery of the new imperial court.

THÉODORE GÉRICAULT (1791-1824)

∧ THE RAFT OF THE MEDUSA

FRANCE, 1816-19
OIL ON CANVAS, H. 4.91 M, W. 7.16 M

Géricault's stark depiction of the crew of a frigate that
foundered off the coast of Senegal caused a scandal,
as had the disaster itself. Due to the incompetence
of the captain, only fifteen of the crew of 149 survived.
Géricault chose the dramatic moment when the survivors,
rising in a pyramid above the dead and dying, hail the
ship that will finally rescue them.

JEAN-AUGUSTE-DOMINIQUE INGRES (1780-1867)

↸ LA GRANDE ODALISQUE

FRANCE, 1814
OIL ON CANVAS, H. 0.91 M, W. 1.62 M

A champion of classicism, Ingres believed firmly in the
supremacy of line over color. He used this Orientalist
evocation of a harem to demonstrate his talent for exotic
and sensual abstraction. His distortion of the female anatomy
and polished style transform the scene into a mysterious icon.

EUGÈNE DELACROIX (1798-1863)

> LIBERTY LEADING THE PEOPLE

FRANCE, 1830
OIL ON CANVAS, H. 2.60 M, W. 3.25 M

In this celebration of the July Revolution, the popular uprising
in July 1830 that brought about the downfall of King Charles X,
Delacroix portrayed Liberty as a woman brandishing the tricolor
flag as she leads the people of Paris over a barricade. His allegory
has become a universal symbol of freedom.

FRANCESCO GUARDI (1712-93)

< **THE BUCENTAUR DEPARTS FOR THE LIDO ON ASCENSION DAY**

ITALY, BETWEEN 1766 AND 1770
OIL ON CANVAS, H. 0.66 M, W. 1.01 M

The election of Doge Alvise IV Mocenigo in 1763 was depicted by Guardi in twelve *vedute* after engravings by Canaletto. This one depicts the symbolic wedding of Venice to the sea (*sposalizio del mare*). Guardi has created a panoramic view of this great port, teeming with activity and architectural marvels, demonstrating his mastery of the representation of space.

JOSEPH MALLARD WILLIAM TURNER (1775-1851)

< **LANDSCAPE WITH A RIVER AND A BAY IN THE DISTANCE**

ENGLAND, C. 1835-40
OIL ON CANVAS, H. 0.93 M, W. 1.23 M

In his late works, some of which he deliberately left unfinished, Turner revolutionized landscape painting by pushing it to the point of abstraction. Using oils almost like watercolor, he created a fusion of forms in a radiant haze of colored light, like memories of the lagoon in Venice.

CASPAR DAVID FRIEDRICH (1774-1840)

> **THE TREE OF CROWS**

GERMANY, 1822
OIL ON CANVAS, H. 59 CM, W. 73 CM

This is not a landscape, or at least not a realistic one, but rather, in the German Romantic spirit that inspired Friedrich, a *vanitas* or reflection on man's fragility. The gnarled branches of an oak growing out of a barren crag and the ghostly crows, lit by the pallid glow of the rising sun, are pagan symbols of death.

PAUL DELAROCHE (1797-1856)
> THE YOUNG MARTYR
FRANCE, 1855
OIL ON CANVAS, H. 1.70 M, W. 1.48 M

Romantic painter Paul Delaroche was as famous in his day as Delacroix. His historical pictures enjoyed great popular success. Delaroche regarded this lyrical scene as "the saddest and most sacred" of his works. A young Christian woman, her hands tied, is thrown in the Tiber. An allegory of martyred innocence, the girl recalls Hamlet's drowned fiancée, Ophelia.

JEAN-BAPTISTE-CAMILLE COROT (1796-1875)
< SOUVENIR OF MORTEFONTAINE
FRANCE, 1864
OIL ON CANVAS, H. 65 CM, W. 89 CM

Corot was one of the first painters to paint outdoors. In the 1850s, he became very interested in photography. His landscapes had a directness and sincerity that were new for the time, although they were not as realistic as they appeared. In the studio, he re-created his impressions of views, reflections, light, and atmosphere with a technique that anticipated Impressionism.

PRINTS AND DRAWINGS

AGOSTINO BUSTI, KNOWN AS IL BAMBAIA
(1483-1548)

∧ PROJECT FOR A TOMB

Italy
Pen and brown and gray ink, gray-brown
wash over stylus underdrawing
h. 53.7 cm, w. 43.9 cm

The motif of the triumphal arch, inspired
by ancient Rome, was frequently used by
Renaissance architects in church facades
and funerary monuments. Christianized
by the presence of Christ giving his
blessing and allegories of Faith and
Charity, this architecture imagined
by a Milanese sculptor is represented
using every artifice of perspective.

MAURICE-QUENTIN DELATOUR (1704-1788)

< PORTRAIT OF THE MARQUISE
DE POMPADOUR

France, 1755 Salon
Pastel with gouache highlights on gray-blue
paper, h. 1.75 m, w. 1.28 m

Delatour imbued the pastel portrait with a
monumentality worthy of easel painting and
a delicacy typical of seventeenth-century
taste. Antoinette Poisson (1721–1764), marquise
de Pompadour, Louis XV's mistress, patron of
the arts and manufactories and an amateur
artist herself, is portrayed surrounded by
publications that she supported, including
Diderot and Alembert's Encyclopédie.

The Department of Prints and Drawings,
the core of which was originally formed
by the royal drawings collection, now
comprises over 140,000 works on paper.
It is one of the finest collections of
miniatures, drawings, prints, watercolors,
pastels, artists' sketchbooks, and
illustrated books in Europe. These are
fragile works that are easily damaged
by light and therefore cannot be put on
permanent display. However, they form
an indispensable adjunct to the paintings
collection and are exhibited in rotating
installations. They can also be viewed by
appointment in the department's study
room in the Flore wing.

The collection is particularly rich
in Italian and French works from the
sixteenth to the nineteenth century.
There are drawings by the greatest
masters, including Leonardo da Vinci,
Raphael, Poussin, Ingres, and Géricault,
while the northern schools are
represented by Dürer, Rembrandt, and
Rubens. There are works in the most
diverse techniques and formats, ranging
from medieval miniatures to Le Brun's
cartoons for the decorative schemes
he designed for Louis XIV and the
sketchbooks Delacroix brought back
from Morocco. The collection was
complemented by the collection
of 40,000 prints and 3,000 drawings
bequeathed by Edmond de Rothschild
in 1935, and by the chalcography collection,
a legacy of the Cabinet du Roi,
comprising over 13,000 plates from the
Renaissance to the twentieth century.

JEAN FOUQUET (C. 1425-C. 1480)

∧ CAESAR'S ARMY CROSSING THE RUBICON

FRANCE, AFTER 1470-75
ILLUMINATION ON VELUM, H. 44 CM, W. 32.5 CM

It was while crossing the border between Roman Italy and Gaul that Emperor
Julius Caesar is said to have uttered the famous words "alea jacta est" (the die
is cast). Jean Fouquet was the greatest French painter of the fifteenth century
and his manuscript illuminations display the same mastery of space and
perspective, which he acquired in Renaissance Italy, as his paintings.

JACOPO BELLINI (1396-1470?)

∧ THE FUNERAL OF THE VIRGIN

ITALY
PEN AND BROWN INK ON PARCHMENT
H. 38 CM, W. 26 CM

This scene of the Virgin's entombment
by the apostles, taken from Jacobus de
Voragine's *Golden Legend*, was part of
a ninety-two-page book already famous
during the Venetian artist's lifetime.
The spatial conception was inspired by
the principles of the humanist architect
Alberti. The alignment of the heads
accentuates the perspective, drawing
the eye toward the fantastic backdrop,
which is still medieval in feeling.

RAFFAELLO SANTI, KNOWN AS RAPHAEL
(1483-1520)

∧ ANNUNCIATION

ITALY
PEN AND BROWN INK, BROWN WASH OVER
BLACK CHALK, H. 28.4 CM, W. 42.3 CM

Drawn between 1499 and 1504, this
was a sketch for one of the paintings
Raphael painted for the altarpiece of
the chapel of the Oddi family at Perugia.
The tripartite architectural structure
evoking the Holy Trinity, centered round
the column symbolizing Christ's Passion,
contrasts with the serenity of the
figures of the Virgin and the angel.

ANTONELLO DA MESSINA (C. 1457-1479)

> GROUP OF FEMALE FIGURES
IN FRONT OF A ROW
OF HOUSES

ITALY, C. 1475
PEN AND BROWN INK, H. 20 CM, W. 21.5 CM

Like many fifteenth-century Italian artists,
this Sicilian painter's naturalistic drawing
was inspired by Flemish masters. In this
rare perspective composition depicting
a secular subject, possibly part of a larger
composition, the architectural setting
is reminiscent of Venice, where Antonello
da Messina lived late in life.

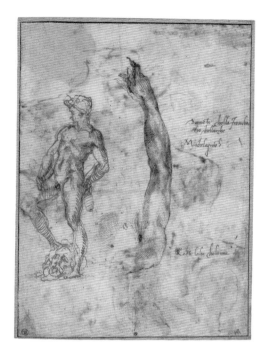

MICHELANGELO BUONARROTI (1475-1564)

< ## STUDIES FOR THE STATUE OF
DAVID AND STUDY OF A LEFT ARM
ITALY
PEN AND BROWN INK, H. 26.2 CM, W. 18.5 CM

David, symbolizing the republic of Florence's resistance to the powerful
Borgia and Medici families, is Michelangelo's most famous work. Both
the preparatory drawings and the marble statue itself illustrate his quest
for ideal beauty through the study of the human figure, particularly male,
and the harmony between the forces of nature and the intellect.

LEONARDO DA VINCI (1452-1519)

∨ ## PORTRAIT OF ISABELLA D'ESTE

ITALY, 1500
BLACK, RED, AND OCHER CHALK, STUMP, WHITE HIGHLIGHTS
H. 61 CM, W. 46.5 CM

This is a study for a portrait of the great humanist princess and patron
of the Renaissance, which Leonardo never painted. The combination of
the frontal bust and head in profile, highly unusual in Leonardo's work,
is a reference to imperial Roman portrait medals. The delicate drawing
of the hands and face is reminiscent of the *Mona Lisa*.

ANTONIO ALLEGRI, KNOWN AS CORREGGIO (1489-1534)

∧ ## ALLEGORY OF THE VICES

ITALY, C. 1530-34
TEMPERA ON CANVAS, H. 1.42 M, W. 0.85 M

Painted, like its pendant dedicated to the
Virtues, for the *studiolo* (a small room or
study housing a collection) of Isabella d'Este
in the ducal palace in Mantua, this moral
allegory illustrates the taste and culture of
the humanist princes. It shows a bearded man,
Dionysos or Silenus, victim of his drunkenness.
Tied to a tree, he is being tormented by
three scantily clad women, each tempting
him in her own way.

GIULIO CAMPAGNOLA (1482-C. 1516)

⌄ TRAVELERS IN A LANDSCAPE WITH A FORTIFIED TOWN ON A ROCK NEAR THE SEA

ITALY
PEN AND BROWN INK, RED CHALK, H. 17.3 CM, W. 26.1 CM

This drawing shows the capacity of draftsmen to assimilate the diverse artistic trends of their time. The village in ruins was a recurrent motif in the work both of northern artists and the Venetian Bellini, while the horizon bounded by a stretch of water comes from the engravings of the German Dürer. The clarity of this drawing is also reminiscent of Mantegna.

PIETER BRUEGHEL THE ELDER (C. 1525-1569)

⌃ ALPINE LANDSCAPE

FLANDERS, 1553
PEN AND BROWN INK, H. 23.6 CM, W. 34.2 CM

Executed during a stay in Italy, this drawing reveals the Flemish painter's fascination for picturesque views, particularly for the grandiose wildness of the Alps. He succeeds in combining a free and harmonious treatment of space and light with the rich detail of the figures, villages, castle, rocks, and trees.

FEDERICO BAROCCI, KNOWN AS BAROCCIO (1535-1612)

^ THE ADORATION OF THE SHEPHERDS

ITALY, C. 1560
PEN AND BROWN INK, BROWN WASH, BLACK CHALK,
WHITE HIGHLIGHTS, GRAY-BLUE PAPER
H. 19.3 CM, W. 25.9 CM

The religious fervor of the Catholic Counter-
Reformation, opposed to the rise of Protestantism,
was a rich period in sacred art. Baroccio was
one of Pope Pius IV's official painters in Rome.
The worship of the Virgin Mary and the saints
pervaded pious images, and Nativities and
Adorations became pretexts for dramatic
nocturnal scenes.

TIZIANO VECELLIO, KNOWN AS TITIAN
(1488/90-1576)

< THE BATTLE OF SPOLETO

ITALY
CHARCOAL AND BLACK CHALK WITH
WHITE HIGHLIGHTS AND BROWN WASH;
SQUARED IN BLACK CHALK
H. 38.1 CM, W. 44.2 CM

This drawing is one of the rare vestiges
of the second commission Titian executed
for the city of Venice after he succeeded
Bellini as its official painter. The battle
between Pope Alexander III and Frederick
Barbarossa in 1155 was the subject of an
enormous mural he painted for the Council
Chamber in the Doges' Palace, completed
in 1538 but destroyed by fire in 1577.

REMBRANDT HARMENSZ. VAN RIJN (1606-1669)

∨ THE THREE CROSSES

HOLLAND
DRYPOINT ON PARCHMENT, H. 38.8 CM, W. 45.6 CM

Chiaroscuro was one of the techniques that Rembrandt used to give
his etchings their extraordinary dramatic intensity. Throughout his
life, he illustrated the Bible with great spirituality and profundity.
In *The Three Crosses*, the most impressive of these compositions,
radiant divine light contrasts with powerful shadows.

CHARLES LE BRUN (1619-1690)

> ## AFRICA

FRANCE
BLACK CHALK AND WHITE HIGHLIGHTS ON BEIGE PAPER
H. 1.78 M, W. 1.95 M

The remarkable Ambassadors' Staircase at Versailles,
designed by architect Louis Le Vau, was given
a sumptuous painted decor on the theme of
the four parts of the world. Le Brun, First Painter
to Louis XIV, drew three hundred life-size cartoons,
all of which have been conserved. This one depicts
Africa as a woman mounting an elephant.

NICOLAS POUSSIN (1594-1665)

v ## APOLLO AND DAPHNE

FRANCE
PEN AND BROWN INK AND BROWN WASH OVER
PREPARATORY SKETCH IN BLACK CHALK
H. 30.9 CM, W. 43 CM

A sketch for the last painting, never finished,
of the most Italian of French painters, this drawing
illustrates the misadventures of Apollo and Daphne,
symbol of unhappy love provoked by Cupid's
revenge. This complex composition, depicting
several moments from the story, emphasizes
meditation rather than action.

JEAN-ANTOINE WATTEAU (1684-1721)

< STUDIES OF EIGHT HEADS, WITH A RIGHT HAND HOLDING A MASK

FRANCE, C. 1715-16
BLACK, RED, AND WHITE CHALK, PASTEL HIGHLIGHTS
H. 26.5 CM, W. 39.7 CM

These drawings of anatomical details are typical of the kind of academic studies undertaken by painters at the time. They are brought to life by the use of three different chalks. Such *pensées*, to use Watteau's term, were sometimes used in paintings, but these are works of art in themselves, illustrating the constant quest for truthfulness.

JACOB JORDAENS (1593-1678)

∨ IVO, PATRON SAINT OF LAWYERS

FLANDERS
TEMPERA ON TWO CARDS STUCK TOGETHER, H. 3 M, W. 3.12 M

Saint Ivo, a lawyer of the poor who lived in the thirteenth century, is depicted here in a seventeenth-century Baroque Flemish interior with a ruined family that is imploring him for aid and is being shown the heavens as a sign of divine providence. This is a cartoon for one of a set of eight tapestries illustrating *Flemish proverbs*, in this case, "Usury is a great sin, a grave plague in the city."

GIANDOMENICO TIEPOLO (1727-1804)

^ JESUS NAILED TO THE CROSS

ITALY
PEN AND BROWN INK, BROWN WASH, H. 48.5 CM, W. 37.5 CM

The son of the famous Venetian painter Giambattista Tiepolo, Giandomenico showed his great gifts as a draftsman in works inspired by biblical subjects. They do not appear to be studies for paintings. Their execution is rapid and spontaneous, but the composition and perspective remain elaborate.

JEAN-ETIENNE LIOTARD (1702-1889)

v PORTRAIT OF MADAME TRONCHIN

SWITZERLAND, 1758
PASTEL, H. 63 CM, W. 50 CM

This Swiss painter and engraver, a master of pastel technique, specialized in portraiture. He faithfully and sensitively captured the likeness and austere expression of Anne de Molène, the wife of a minister. The rigor of her Calvinist education is evident in the sobriety and discreet luxury of her clothes and intelligent gaze.

GIOVANNI BATTISTA PIRANESI, KNOWN AS PIRANESI (1720-1778)

< PALACE INTERIOR

ITALY; PEN AND BROWN INK, BROWN WASH, RED CHALK
H. 51.2 CM, W. 76.5 CM

This is an early work by the Venetian artist who became famous for his views of imaginary architecture, particularly his series showing prisons, which circulated as engravings. This large drawing typifies his visionary approach, which his consummate mastery of wash drawing imbued with a grandiose dimension. A celebration in honor of a hero is the pretext here for a theatrical treatment of architectural space.

ANNE-LOUIS GIRODET DE ROUSSY-TRIOSON
(1767-1824)

> ### THE JUDGMENT OF MIDAS

FRANCE
BLACK CHALK, BISTER AND GRAY WASH,
PEN AND BROWN INK, WHITE HIGHLIGHTS
H. 30.2 CM, W. 49.8 CM

Girodet, a pupil of David, brought a taste
for the strange and bizarre to Neoclassicism.
He drew his subject matter from classical
authors, legends, and even contemporary
writers such as Chateaubriand. The thematic
complexity of this scene from Ovid's
Metamorphoses is conveyed with great
clarity by his fine, tight drawing.

PIERRE-PAUL PRUD'HON (1758-1823)

< ### WEALTH

FRANCE
BLACK CHALK AND WHITE HIGHLIGHTS
ON BLUE PAPER
H. 3.10 M, W. 0.75 M

Between 1797 and 1801, Prud'hon
was commissioned to decorate
two reception rooms in the Parisian
mansion of the financier Lannoy,
one on the theme of the four seasons,
the second consisting of four large
panels with female figures symbolizing
wealth, the arts, the pleasures,
and philosophy. This life-size
cartoon for wealth is full of
allegories to antiquity.

JEAN-AUGUSTE-DOMINIQUE INGRES (1780-1867)

< ### PORTRAIT OF THE STAMATY FAMILY

FRANCE
GRAPHITE, H. 46.3 CM, W. 37.1 CM

Portrait drawings, in this case of the family of
the French consul in Rome during the Empire,
were undertaken as full-fledged works in their own
right, in the English tradition, and were a valuable
source of income for a young artist. Graphite
enabled Ingres to draw the outlines with great
precision and create subtle shading.

ARTS OF ASIA, AFRICA, OCEANIA, AND THE AMERICAS

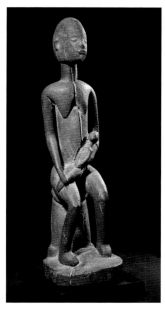

MASTER OF THE RED MATERNITY
MOTHER AND CHILD
Dogon Plateau, Mali, 14th century
Wood, h. 75 cm

The universal and sacred theme of the mother and child has always been an important one for African sculptors. Effigies like this one are fertility symbols, as well as being tributes to the "Wives of the Beyond," to the femininity of female ancestors. The gentleness and serenity of this work are universal.

DIVINATION BOX
Central Ivory Coast
Second half of the 19th century
Wood, terracotta, h. 25 cm

This extraordinary mouse divination box is the work of the artist Baoulé. A figurine of a meditating witch doctor is leaning against a large stone jar in which was placed a mouse, an inhabitant of the sacred netherworld of the ancestors, together with sticks bearing pieces of fruit, whose changing positions enabled one to predict future events.

> ## STATUETTE OF A SEATED MAN
Northern Luzon, Philippines, 15th century
Wood, h. 48 cm

This superbly balanced Ifugao sculpture has the exceptional sense of stylized proportion that is the hallmark of the funerary art of the earliest inhabitants of the Philippine islands. The sculpture of this seafaring people was related to its tradition of oral literature in which animist epics played an important part.

< ## FANG RELIQUARY FIGURE
Equatorial Guinea or Gabon, mid-19th century
Wood, h. 60 cm

The most powerful art forms in African art are masks and figures. This statuette was acquired in the nineteenth century by the Musée d'Ethnographie du Trocadéro. The skillful organization of stylized forms that inspired Cubism was used here to express spirituality. Ancestor figures were the intercessors between the world of the living and spirits.

The Louvre was already a "museum of distant lands" in the nineteenth century. During the Second Republic, an ethnographic "Oriental and African" museum and an "American" museum of Pre-Columbian antiquities were opened on the second floor of the Cour Carrée. These complemented the Musée de la Marine, founded in 1827, also rich in ethnographic collections. In 1878, these collections joined the ethnographic museum in the Palais du Trocadéro, the future Musée de l'Homme, where they remained until the end of the twentieth century, while the Asian art collections were transferred to the Musée Guimet in 1945.

In conjunction with the decision to group the collections of so-called "primitive" art together in the new Musée du Quai Branly in Paris, it was also decided to present a selection of masterpieces from Asia, Africa, Oceania, and the Americas in the Louvre. These works, for the most part sculptures in wood, together with pieces in bronze, ivory, terracotta, and stone, testify to the spirituality and artistic creation of civilizations that were for a long time regarded as inferior, despite the major role they played in revolutionizing Western art through the work of Gauguin, Breton, Picasso, Giacometti, and others. The display in the Louvre offers a unique opportunity to juxtapose the forms and ideas of Western art with the hieratic quality of African sculpture, the strangeness of the idols of the Pacific islands, and the diversity of Mesoamerican civilizations—Maya, Inca, and Aztec—and North American cultures, such as the Inuit.

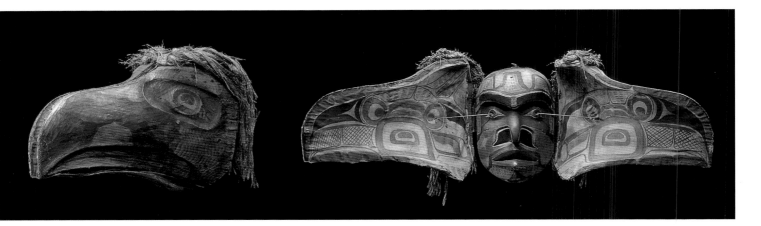

∧ TRANSFORMATION MASK

BRITISH COLUMBIA, CANADA, 19TH CENTURY
WOOD, H. 0.34 M, W. 1.30 M (OPEN)

This spectacular mask from the northwest coast of Alaska once belonged to Claude Lévi-Strauss. An example of the magical and dreamlike art of the Kwakiutl, this man's head enclosed within the skull of a tutelary bird would have played a terrifying role during ritual ceremonies and hypnotized the audience with its multiple eyes.

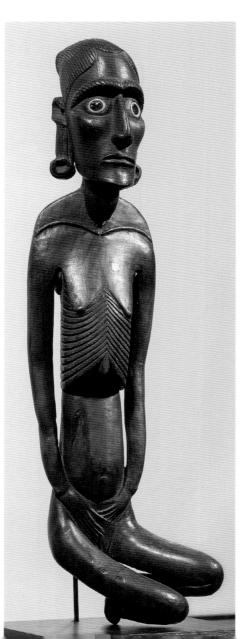

> POST OF A CEREMONIAL HOUSE

SAN CRISTÓBAL, SOLOMON ISLANDS
17TH CENTURY
WOOD, H. 2.11 M

The pantheon of Oceanic divinities and the scenes depicted on the large posts of ceremonial houses can be surprising for Westerners. This stylized carving of two ancestors copulating had both symbolic and ritual significance.

< MALE FIGURE

EASTER ISLAND, 17TH-18TH CENTURY
WOOD, H. 34 CM

Oceanic sculpture is very diverse and Polynesian, Melanesian, and Micronesian artists gave free rein to their imaginations to give us disconcerting, magical images that are often incomprehensible when removed from their original context. The small wooden *moai kavakava* statues of Easter Island are thought to represent male ancestors. They are characterized by their emaciated appearance and prominent rib cages, and they have the same huge eyes as the island's famous stone statues.

> WHISTLE STATUETTE

LATE CLASSIC PERIOD, JAINA ISLAND,
CAMPECHE, MEXICO, 7TH-10TH CENTURY
TERRACOTTA, 19.3 CM

With its almond eyes, well-defined lips, and aquiline nose, this figure's face conforms to the Maya canon of beauty. The figure wears a tiara, which covers the ritual damage inflicted on its skull. This is a rare peaceful image from a civilization that was dominated by violence and human sacrifice.

PHOTO CREDITS

Musée du Louvre
Henri Loyrette > *President and Director*
Didier Selles > *Executive Director*

Aline Sylla-Walbaum > *Assistant Executive Director,*
Head of Cultural Development

Éditions du Musée du Louvre
Violaine Bouvet-Lanselle >
Head of Publications,
Department of Cultural Development, Musée du Louvre
With the collaboration of Isabelle Calvi

Éditions Hazan
Editor > Bernard Wooding
Designer > Sylvie Milliet
Designer (cover) > Jean-Marc Barrier
Production Manager > Claire Hostalier

Translated from the French by David Wharry

© Musée du Louvre, Paris, 2006
© Éditions Hazan, Paris, 2006

http://www.louvre.fr

ISBN Louvre > 2 35031 057 4
ISBN Hazan > 2 7541 0069 5
Achevé d'imprimer > juillet 2015

Photoengraving > IGS, l'Isle-d'Espagnac, France
Printed in France by Pollina, Luçon - n° L73156

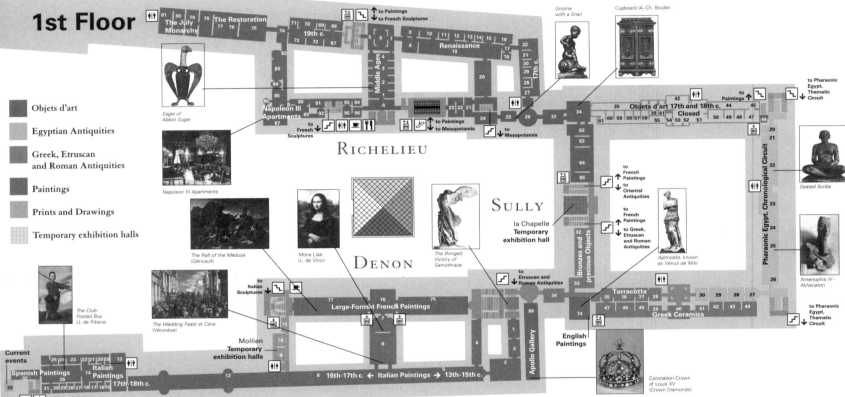

1st Floor

The July Monarchy · 81 80 79 78 · The Restoration · 77 76 75

71 70 69 68 · 74 · 19th c. · 73 72 67

to Paintings
to French Sculptures

5 · 4 · 6 · 9 10 · 11 12 · 13 14 · 15 · 16

Middle Ages · 3 2 1 A

Renaissance · 19 · 17 18 · 30 31 · 32 · 7th c.

20 · 29 28 27

Gnome with a Snail

Cupboard (A.-Ch. Boulle)

82 83 84 85 86

Napoleon III Apartments · 90 91 · 92 · 89 · 95 96 · 87 93 94

23 22 21 · 24 · 25 26 · 33 · 34

to French Sculptures

to Paintings
to Mesopotamia

to Mesopotamia

42 · to Paintings

to Pharaonic Egypt, Thematic Circuit

Objets d'art 17th and 18th c. · Closed · 44 45

61 · 60 59 58 57 56 · 55 54 53 52 51 · 50 49 48 47 · 46

35 · 38 41

20 21 22 23 24 25 26

Seated Scribe

Amenophis IV - Akhenaton

Pharaonic Egypt, Chronological Circuit

Objets d'art
Egyptian Antiquities
Greek, Etruscan and Roman Antiquities
Paintings
Prints and Drawings
Temporary exhibition halls

Eagle of Abbot Suger

Napoleon III Apartments

RICHELIEU

62 63 64 65

la Chapelle Temporary exhibition hall

to French Paintings
to Oriental Antiquities

to French Paintings
to Greek, Etruscan and Roman Antiquities

S U L L Y

The Raft of the Medusa (Géricault)

Mona Lisa (L. de Vinci)

The Winged Victory of Samothrace

Aphrodite, known as Vénus de Milo

DENON

32 33 34

Bronzes and precious Objects

The Club-Footed Boy (J. de Ribera)

The Wedding Feast at Cana (Véronèse)

to Italian Sculptures

to Etruscan and Roman Antiquities

Large-Format French Paintings · 77 76 75

35 36 37 38 · 30 29 28 27

Terracotta

47 46 45 44 · 40 41 42 43 44

Greek Ceramics

74

to Pharaonic Egypt, Thematic Circuit

Mollien Temporary exhibition halls

11 · 10 · 9 · 7 · 6 · 5 · 4 · 1 2 3

66

Apollo Gallery

English Paintings

Current events

Spanish Paintings · 25 24 23 · 22 21 20 19 · 13 · Italian Paintings · 14 · 17th-18th c.

32 · 26 · 31 30 29 28 27 18 17 16 15 · 12

33

towards Exit
Porte des Lions

8 · 16th-17th c. ← Italian Paintings → 13th-15th c. · 5

Coronation Crown of Louis XV (Crown Diamonds)